THE Chaplaincy

THE Chaplaincy

Chaplain Certification Program

Dale Scadron

Author Reputation Press LLC
45 Dan Road Suite 5
Canton MA 02021
www.authorreputationpress.com
Hotline: 1(800) 220-7660
Fax: 1(855) 752-6001

Ordering Information:
Quantity sales. Special discounts are available on quantity purchases by corporations, associations, and others. For details, contact the publisher at the address above.

Printed in the United States of America.

ISBN-13:	Softcover	978-1-64961-757-6
	eBook	978-1-64961-758-3

Library of Congress Control Number: 2021917250

CLASS OUTLINE

CHAPLAIN DUTIES

Lesson 1 - Introduction to Industrial Chaplaincy.......... 3

- Pastor vs Chaplain
- Chaplains in Law Enforcement Overview
- The Fire Chaplain Overview
- Prison Ministry Overview
- The Hospital Chaplain Overview
- The Hospice Chaplain Overview
- The Corporate Chaplain Overview
- The Three Levels of Chaplaincy
- Ecclesiastical Endorsement
- The Professional Paid Chaplain
- The Volunteer / Reserve Chaplain
- Visitation Chaplains

Lesson 2 - Chaplain/Volunteers in the Prisons 15

- When Arrested
- Maximum Security Inmates
- Comparative Chaplain Duties
- Prison Rape Elimination Act (PREA)
- Definition of Sexual Misconduct
- PREA Reporting Laws
- Response Protocols Page
- When to Activate the Alarm
- Preservation of Evidence
- Victims vs. Perpetrators
- Dynamics of Sexual Abuse / Harassment in Confinement
- Common Reactions of Victims of Sexual Abuse / Harassment

- Communicating with the Victim
- The Anatomy of a Setup
- How to Prevent Boundary Violations
- Self-Evaluation

Lesson 3 - Duties of the Emergency Service 31

- Agency Confidentiality
- A Ministry of Presence
- Providing Comfort during Crisis and Trauma
- Officer Involved Shootings
- In the Line of Duty Death
- Visit Sick or Injured
- Callouts and War-Bags
- Crisis Intervention Overview
- Notifying next-of-kin in death or serious injury incidents
- Victim Assistances
- Spiritual Guidance and Care   Page
- Special Events

Lesson 4 - Emergency Protocols 43

- Command Structure
- Emergency Call Outs
- Providing information
- Incident Command Protocols
- Prison Riots
- Arriving on the scene of a Traffic Accident
- The Communicating the right way
- Ride Along
- Radio Traffic

Lesson 5 - Pastoral Confidentiality and Ethics 51

- Confidentiality - Case History

- Mandated Reporter
- Gratuity and Favors
- Chaplain Badge and Uniform

Lesson 6 - Dealing with Suicidal People 59

- Suicide Callouts and on Scene Protocols
- The Jumper or Man with a Gun
- Attempted Suicide - Do's & Don'ts
- Zone of Safety
- Common Misconceptions about Suicide
- Asking Key Questions Page
- Look for warning signs

Lesson 7 - Death Notifications 69

- In Person
- Time and Certainty
- Notifications in Pairs
- Use Plain Language
- Compassion during Crisis
- What not to say
- Viewing the body
- Workplace Notifications
- Hospital Notifications
- Debrief the Chaplain
- Notification Specific to Suicide
- Survivors Response

BIBLICAL COUNSELING

Lesson 8 - Biblical Counseling 101 81

- Spiritual Counseling vs. Psychology
- Common Reasons for Seeking Counseling

- There are Two Major Reasons for Seeking Counseling
- There are two goals in Biblical counseling
- There are Two Major Types of Counselees
- The Five –Step process of Biblical Counseling

Lesson 9 - The Building Blocks of Counseling.............. 91

- The Three Building Blocks needed to build a Relationship during Counseling
- How empathize with others
- Use Appropriate Non-Verbal Communication

Lesson 10 - Gathering Information Part 1.................. 101

- Listening and Observing the Counselee
- The Need to Gather Facts
- Digging Deeper
- Active Listing
- Listen Beyond Attitudes and Feelings
- Control the Flow of the Talk

Lesson 11–Gathering Information Part 2.................... 115

- What is Halo Data?
- Learning about a Person from Body Language
- Material for Questions
- Productive Questioning

Lesson 12 - Personal Assessment Forms...................... 127

- Information Collection Tools
- Personal Discovery Assignment Form (PDA)
- Marriage and Family Information
- Discovering Problem Patterns (DPP)
- Taking Thoughts Captive Worksheet

Lesson 13- Biblical Process of Change 139

- Carnal Feelings vs. God's Will
- Taking Responsibility
- Elements of True Repentance
- Renewal of Mind
- Maintaining Change

CRISIS INTERVENTION

Lesson 14- Critical Situational Stress 165

- Dealing with a Recent Death
- What is Critical Situational Stress?
- Counseling during Critical Stress
- Preparatory Checklist for Debriefing
- Phases of Debriefing
- Common Immediate Stress Reactions
- Symptoms during a Crisis

Lesson 15 - Traumatic Stress Reactions and Children 173

- Three Basic Postures
- Key Points when Dealing with Children's Grief
- Children / Post Crisis Behaviors Page
- Symptoms from Crisis
- Ways Parents Can Help Their Children

DEALING WITH DEATH AND DYING

Lesson 16 - Grief and Bereavement.......................... 181

- Grief comes in Waves
- Obsession with the Death

- Definitions, a quick checklist
- Reactions to Grief
- When to Make a Referral

Lesson 17 - Preparing for Approaching Death......... 187

- If they die today, are they ready to meet Jesus?
- Normal Physiological Signs and Symptoms during the
- Final Stages of Life
- Giving Permission
- Saying Good-Bye
- Bedside manners
- Things to know About the Dying
- Habits of Effective Comforters

Lesson 18 - Healing Conversations............................ 193

- Four steps to the Conversation Process
- What to when counseling the bereaved
- Communicating with those in Grief
- What to Say and What not to Say

<u>COUNSELING RECAP</u>

Information at a Glance..200

- Collecting and Organizing Data
- Taking Notes When Appropriate
- Kind of Information to Collect
- Physical Condition

VALUABLE RESOURCES..207

CHAPLAINS INTERNATIONAL
ENDORSED TRAINING PROGRAM

Published by Chaplains College Press

LICENSE TO USE POLICY

License to use courseware, video and PowerPoint programs and qualified instructors' certificates are available to ministry organizations, churches, bible institutes and bible colleges. Inquiries about licensing should be made by emailing chaplain2000@aol.com or by calling (888) 627-5503 for more information.

Acknowledgements

SPECIAL THANKS TO THE FACULTY OF

Chaplains College School
of Graduate Studies

Earn your certification today by contacting
Chaplains International, Inc.

Chaplains College School of Graduate Studies

Chaplaincy Training Institute

College Board of Examiners

Be it known by all men these presents

John A. Smith

having honorably fulfilled all the requirements as instructed by the instructors of this institution, having completed 20 hours of instruction on the following topics, The Philosophy of Chaplaincy, Core Values, Roles and Responsibilities, Rules Governing Confidentiality, Ethics, Basic Christian Counseling and Crisis Intervention, the Board of Examiners do therefore confer the certificate of

Basic Chaplain Certification (BCC)

in witness whereof, the said organization has caused this Certificate to be approved and signed by the Board of Examiners and the seal of Chaplains College School of Graduate Studies to be hereunto affixed.

Issued August 25th in the year of our Lord 2019

Board of Examiners	Board of Examiners
Board of Examiners	Board of Examiners

Graduate Seal

Author and Senior Instructor

Chaplain Dale A. Scadron, M.Div., Th.D.

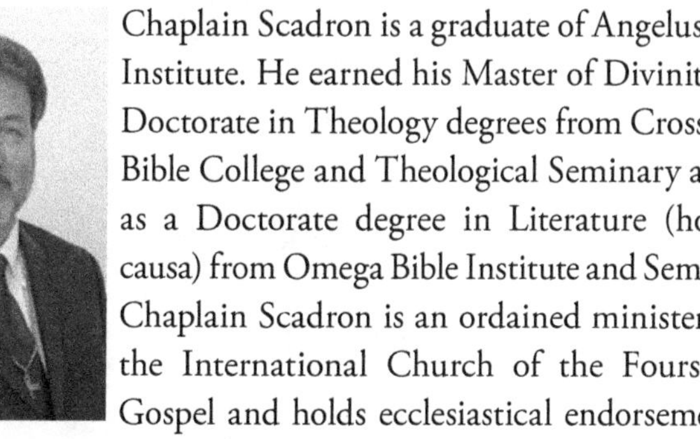

Chaplain Scadron is a graduate of Angelus Bible Institute. He earned his Master of Divinity and Doctorate in Theology degrees from Crossroads Bible College and Theological Seminary as well as a Doctorate degree in Literature (honoris causa) from Omega Bible Institute and Seminary. Chaplain Scadron is an ordained minister with the International Church of the Foursquare Gospel and holds ecclesiastical endorsement as an institutional chaplain. Chaplain Scadron is founder and president of Chaplains International, Inc., founder and chancellor of Chaplains College School of Graduate Studies and founder of the Chaplaincy Training Institute. Chaplain Scadron served, as a fulltime senior chaplain with the Kern County Sheriff Detentions Bureau and was instrumental in the development of the law enforcement chaplains program. Chaplain Scadron served five years as divisional chaplain with the Los Angeles Police Department and eight years as a chaplain for the Glendale Police Department in Glendale California. He served on staff as a chaplain and Volunteer Coordinator at the Taft Federal Correctional Institution located in Taft, California.

Preface

The purpose of this book is to present the reader with a basic but comprehensive view of the work and ministry of the chaplain and provide basics insights to Christian Biblical Counseling. The work of the chaplain is often misunderstood within the sphere of ministry, and all too often churches minimize the role the chaplain plays in the lives of people who are experiencing a crisis. Some church leaders liken chaplaincy to a church outreach rather than a ministry appointment, yet in the world of paid chaplaincy and sometimes volunteer chaplaincy the educational and certification requirements are much higher than that required by most church pastorates.

When I started my work as a police department chaplain back in 1995, I had no experience whatsoever in this area of ministry, and like so many chaplains who started their careers quickly learned the ways of the street through the school of hard knocks. Few bible colleges if any provided any real-world training other than the traditional studies in evangelism that meet a ministerial need but failed to meet any industrial or crisis need. There is sometimes the assumption among industry personnel that if you are designated to serve as a chaplain, the implication is that you are fully qualified to perform your respective duties. It is far from the truth, even the most educated among professional chaplains will often lack specific skillsets required for duty until they are fully acclimated into the role they serve.

A church pastor may never be required to respond to a crime scene where there are fatalities or encounter people who are hysterical with grief. However, a chaplain depending upon his or her assignment may encounter such tragedies. The responding mechanism to such events may be far different from that of the pastor. For example, when dealing with a family member (s) of someone who commits suicide, who succumbs to a shotgun blast to the head, it is natural for the minister to go into a pastoral mode, assuring the victim that everything will be all right as long as they remain faithful. The pastor may overlook the monolithic conditions of the event that has just occurred. Not everything is going to be all right, an irreversible tragedy has just occurred, lives have been dramatically changed forever, and not everyone is presumed religious. Therefore, the response may be inappropriate. I am not minimizing faith or questioning the ability of God to bring about good out of an emotionally polarizing situation. However, the skilled chaplain understands there are levels of human emotions that may occur during the moments of tragedy and platitudes while quick and easy can often cause irrevocable damage. Understanding the culture, the life of those who serve in various industries will help the minister to adapt to the environment where he or she has chosen to minister and become an asset rather than a hindrance.

A great deal of time has been given to the second portion of this book covering the topic of Biblical Counseling, which is a foundational course within Chaplains College School of Graduate Studies in, and of itself. The program is foundational, because all levels of chaplaincy are based upon the ability of the person to perform his or her duties as a chaplain, as well as an effective communicator and caregiver. In this book, we will use the nouthetic approach (developed by Dr. Jay Adams) to biblical counseling, using the Bible as our primary source for addressing emotional needs. Labeled a ministry of presence, when the need arises, the minister must be ready to address spiritual and emotional trauma both through verbal and no-verbal communication. After completing this course, we hope that you will walk away with a greater understanding and respect for the work of the chaplain.

Dale A. Scadron Th.D.

Chaplain Dale A. Scadron, M.Div., Th.D.

Part 1

Surviving In The World Of Chaplaincy

Lesson 1

Introduction to Industrial Chaplaincy

Pastor vs Chaplain

Institutional Chaplaincy is a ministry that is unique and varied. Institutional chaplains serve correctional facilities, police and fire agencies, medical centers, senior-care, universities, and colleges. Pastors and Chaplains share many tasks and competencies. Both have experienced a special call to ministry and service. Both are teachers, caregivers, witnesses of their faith, and advocates for people. Both have a desire to equip people to grow in spiritual maturity. So, one might ask, what is the difference? Perhaps the most significant difference is the setting in which the ministry is provided. Congregational Pastors usually minister to a group of people who have similar religious beliefs and share many common cultural identities, such as language, geographic location, socioeconomic status, or ethnic identity.

Chaplains, on the other hand, usually minister to a group of people of many different religious beliefs or no religious beliefs at all. These people usually represent many different cultural identities. Within the church, the local congregation or ecclesiastical body gives the church pastor authority. In contrast, Chaplains are given authority by the institution that employs them in addition to the ecclesiastical body that endorses them. Chaplains are clergy members from various religious faiths who have chosen to minister to a group of people outside the church walls. From a Christian perspective, their role is pastoral, prophetic, and priestly, even while being nonreligious to those who profess no religion. They enter into ministry with no personal agenda and the attitude of a servant.

Christian Chaplains are an extension of Christ's ministry to all people. There is a common misconception that Chaplains have left the real ministry to do social ministry, yet it is far from the truth. Jesus did make a habit of regular synagogue attendance, and He often taught there (Luke 4:16-24). However, most of His ministry was very much outside the walls of the institutional "church." He taught on the seashore, on mountaintops, over dinner tables, and along the roads as He walked. Additionally, He did not limit His ministry to devout Jews, but befriended sinners and tax collectors, healed Romans and Samaritans. He preached to crowds of mixed Jewish and Gentile ancestry.

Following Christ's example of cross-cultural ministry, Chaplains provide care and compassion to working professionals. Jesus taught that all people have value in the eyes of God, not just those who shared His ethnicity, culture, and religion. Jesus taught that if people wanted to be considered righteous and "inherit the kingdom" of God, they were to minister to all people, notably those considered the least of society. They are the homeless, the disabled, the uneducated, and the terminally ill.

Additionally, however, Chaplains face the challenge of providing loving care to all they encounter, even those whose social or economic status does not seem to warrant help or those whose celebrity status already commands attention or assistance. Other times the challenge is providing and demonstrating God's love to those who do not seem to deserve care and compassion, particularly perpetrators of a heinous crime or people who are a threat to Christianity. Chaplains follow God's example by loving and caring for any person regardless of age, gender, culture, race, color, or ethnic background. There is undoubtedly biblical precedence for taking ministry to the people rather than waiting for them to attend church.

The Chaplain's mandate is to be involved in the crisis of people's lives, regardless of personal religious convictions. The Chaplain is often in the position of ministering to the basic needs of others. That ministry is not a hook to obligate the person to attend religious services. Ministry is provided without conditions or expectations. It should be out of genuine love and compassion. The Chaplain must always exercise wisdom in choosing the appropriate ministry intervention for each situation. Attending to the physical needs of people in crisis must precede evangelism. People who are hurting perceive a greater need to stop the pain and suffering and may not be open to proselytizing. Hungry and hurting people find little comfort in religious tracts and platitudes when they need basic necessities. Jesus made ministry practical in order to make evangelism possible. James 2:14-17 states that by our good works (deeds), others would be able to see the genuineness of our faith.

The Chaplain, as a representative or ambassador of Christ, is privileged to stay with someone during times of emotional and physical suffering, without trying to fix the person's problems, offer unsolicited advice, or recite religious platitudes. Being present in a time of crisis offers tremendous moral support. The fact that the Chaplain is there may enable them to believe that God has not abandoned them and communicates God's assurance. The book of Isaiah reassures us, *"Fear not, for I am with you."* (Isaiah 41:10, NKJV)[1]*By (CI) Chaplain Norberto Guzman, B.A., M.C.C. / Chaplains College School of Graduate Studies/ Special resource: www.coursehero.com*[2]

Different Roles of Chaplains

Chaplains in Law Enforcement Overview

Law enforcement Chaplains serve municipal law enforcement agencies, such as city police or county sheriffs. They also do state agencies that include park rangers, state patrol, and highway patrol. In addition to these entities, there is a broader field in federal agencies that provides for the Secret Service, the FBI, and U.S. Border Patrol.

Chaplains are often assigned to perform their duties at a designated location and serve at a divisional level. Law enforcement Chaplains have many responsibilities related directly to officers and general personnel of the law enforcement agencies. For example, the Chaplain may ride with officers while on duty, attend roll calls, departmental meetings, and provide counseling for officers and family members. They are often called upon to visit officers and departmental personnel who are hospitalized or homebound.

Chaplains in law enforcement have many duties that relate to victims within the community. In this arena, they counsel victims of crime and provide them with spiritual care. In the event of a disaster where large communities have been majorly affected, families need someone to aid them and direct them thru the chaos they have endured. Chaplains visit them, counsel the families, and bring them comfort. Spiritual care in the aftermath of a major disaster can be feeding the hungry, clothing the naked, providing water for the thirsty, or sheltering the exposed. Again, restating that once the person's immediate needs are met, they will be more likely to discuss their spiritual needs. Law enforcement Chaplains fill a unique role in providing spiritual care, religious ministry, and intercession in the lives of many officers and support personnel who serve the public in crises and stressful situations.[3]

Chaplains may be the only spiritual provider many officers and staff will ever know. With compassion, experience, and common sense, Chaplains counsel and encourage through availability, presence, non-judgmental listening, and building trusting relationships by being dependable, honest, and transparent. Many agencies require specialized training. Some requirements may include training in First Aid, CPR, and critical incident stress management training. Each agency has its needs, and even the experienced Chaplain may be required to go thru the agency's orientation training program. *By (CI) Chaplain Norberto Guzman, B.A., M.C.C. / Chaplains College School of Graduate Studies/Special Resource: bcnn1wp.wordpress.com*

The Fire Chaplain Overview

Many fire agencies recruit local clergy to serve as volunteer chaplains to handle emergencies within the department. The issues surrounding firefighters are similar to that of those who serve in law enforcement. Duties include performing death notifications, counseling department personnel and their families, and being available to minister during times of crisis. Fire chaplains also conduct weddings and funerals on behalf of Fire personnel, as well as invocations and benedictions at academy graduations. Often, firefighter's tensions are heightened by the long hours spent in the fire station away from their families. The fire service becomes the second family for the firefighter adding stressors to the emergency responder's life. Firefighters compete against their fellow firefighters for advancement. Shift work often leads to an increase in tensions. The adrenaline is continually flowing because they are on duty for days at a time. This factor alone increases stresses as firefighters try to deal with each other and the public.[4]

Prison Ministry Overview

The difference between inmates and the average citizen is that inmates experience these things in complete isolation, separated from loved ones and support systems. The very nature of the circumstances makes them more vulnerable to emotional and spiritual distress. The environment within the correctional institution breeds many issues that intensify with the institution's security level. Jails, prisons, and penitentiaries all deal with inmates who succumb to peer pressure while confined. The correctional minister is continually dealing with the fear inmates have of being perceived as weak and exposed because they have chosen to make a lifestyle change, abandoning the life of criminal activity.[5]

Inmates also deal with issues of depersonalization and dehumanization. They fear breaches of confidentiality, prejudice, and discrimination. For some, fear is the natural outcome of the impending release, resettlement, or even execution. Correctional ministers have the difficult task of building trust with inmates by personalizing their relationships, humanizing their circumstances, equalizing their perceived inequities, and fostering peace and reconciliation...[6]

The correctional institution's environment is often a microcosm of the world of crime outside the bars, guarded walls, and monitored rooms of prison. Thus, the inexperienced chaplain needs to understand prison gangs' criminal nature, sexual assault within the correctional system, drugs, and institutional crime. These are frequent issues inside prison walls, as well as in the world beyond. While ministering to inmates, Chaplains are called by God to provide compassionate care for people. They constantly assess and decide what approach to take, respecting the institutional boundaries that separate the correctional worker from the inmate.

How do chaplains deal with this tension, and by what standards do they function? While the answer may sound cliche, the chaplain may have no choice but to demonstrate their faith by their actions rather than proselytizing the incarcerated. The prison Chaplain is committed to proclaiming the message of God's love to a people that may have never been to a church or heard God's word before. Taking the initiative to meet people in their pain and suffering requires courage and a desire to change people's lives. Chaplains intentionally choose to enter the lives of the incarcerated, accompanying them on a journey that may include hardship as well as joy. The prison Chaplain enters an environment of differing cultures, interests, and religions. Therefore, the chaplain needs to have integrity and be compassionate. The work of a prison Chaplain begins with God's call to ministry. *By (CI) Chaplain Norberto Guzman, B.A., M.C.C. / Signet Bible College and Theological Seminary*

The Hospital Chaplain Overview

Hospital Chaplains offer ministry and spiritual guidance to patients, family members, and caregivers within the hospital setting. Many Hospital Chaplains work in an interfaith environment using a non-denominational style of counseling. They may perform specific religious duties related to the faith they were ordained in, for example, performing last rites. Chaplains work with a diverse population, counseling patients undergoing surgical procedures, facing "end of life" issues, or involved in a traumatic accident. They also offer comfort and support to the family of patients. Hospital staff may call upon chaplains to calm angry or emotionally distraught friends and family members of patients. Chaplains may conduct religious services in the hospital chapel, including officiating at memorial services and weddings. In some cases, a Hospital Chaplain will provide spiritual support to fellow staff members and other healthcare providers. [7]

The Hospice Chaplain Overview

Hospice chaplain duties pertain to the end-of-life needs of dying patients and their families, caregivers, community, and even the interdisciplinary medical team. Hospice is more than just providing medical interventions during the end of life. Hospice Chaplains provide direct spiritual support and end-of-life counsel to patients and families in keeping with the patient and family's spiritual beliefs. The goal of hospice care is to enable patients to die with dignity, without pain, which includes meeting spiritual needs and social needs. [8]

The Corporate Chaplain Overview

Some businesses, large or small, employ chaplains for their staff and clientele. According to The Economist (August 25, 2007, edition, pg. 64), 4,000 corporate chaplains serve in corporate America. Other chaplaincies outside of emergency services can be found in rodeos, racetracks, fairgrounds, truck stops, clubs, and lodges. Typically, chaplains serve in these specific venues on a volunteer basis and are asked to perform various duties such as invocations at events, officiating weddings, and funerals, and ministering to personnel and their families. Truck driving chaplains often drive large rigs from truck stop to truck stop conducting church services for long-haul drivers. Usually, the trailer converts into a portable open platform allowing weary travelers to participate in church services while away from home. As in the emergency service community, the chaplain spends time with personnel developing relationships and provides spiritual counseling to those in need.

The Three Levels of Chaplaincy

There is often the debate of what defines a professional chaplain and the expectation and role they should play in ministry. It is unfortunate that in some church organizations, the chaplain's role is viewed as less important than that of a church pastor. The church pastor may be unaware of the onerous mandates, endorsement, and educational requirements placed on the chaplain who is seeking full-time employment. There are strict mandates and conditions for the volunteer chaplain as well. There are differences in duties a full-time chaplain must perform vs. a volunteer chaplain for apparent reasons. When monetary compensation is involved, the employer has the freedom to dictate policies and procedures for their chaplains.

Ecclesiastical Endorsement

Ecclesiastical Endorsement is similar to accreditation and is a process by which a denomination or ministry organization certifies to the requesting agency that they wholeheartedly support and validate the chaplain's qualifications and expertise. Should the chaplain fail to meet the employer's expectations or breach institutional protocols, the sponsoring organization will bear some responsibility. Most federal and state governments and healthcare organizations require endorsement as a prerequisite for paid employment. For a denomination or ministry organization to provide a government-recognized endorsement, they must go through a strict governmental registration process and spend thousands of dollars in registration fees. Many independent churches and ministry organizations cannot afford the cost associated with becoming an accredited endorsing agency, so they forgo the process and use an independent endorser for their ministers. Some churches will provide their ministers with an in-house endorsement which may or may not be acceptable to government and healthcare organizations. Generally speaking, Ecclesiastical Endorsement is not required by governmental agencies (Military excluded) for voluntary positions. However, licensing or ordination is usually a minimum requirement for most all public service agencies.

The Professional Paid Chaplain

As mentioned above, most hospitals, state and federal agencies require their chaplains to have Ecclesiastical Endorsement and a minimum of a Master of Divinity Degree (There are some exceptions) to function as a chaplain. Local law enforcement and fire departments tend to be more liberal on the matter and forgo the need for endorsement and higher education. While hospice care facilities may or may not require Clinical Pastoral Education training (CPE) in addition to their educational requirements, in most cases, all hospitals throughout the US do require CPE for paid employment. Again, volunteers are not under the same mandates.

The Volunteer / Reserve Chaplain

Local agencies generally do not require ecclesiastical endorsement or a graduate degree since they classify their chaplains as police reserve or volunteer personnel. It is difficult to ask the local pastor of a congregation to volunteer their time and prequalify for a chaplain's position with a graduate degree when there is no compensation for time and effort. Ironically, emergency services chaplains (usually a volunteer position) are often exposed to crises such as shootings, suicides, and in the line of duty deaths. At times, they face physical dangers, while a full-time paid chaplain (I.e., prison and hospital) may never be exposed to the same level of stress.

The emergency services chaplain will periodically receive ongoing training in crisis management and safety to meet emergency services demands. The hospital or prison chaplain will rarely be required to respond to crises other than what takes place within the hospital or prison setting. Though the emergency service chaplain is a non-compensated position, they are still classified as non-paid professionals. In comparison, a reserve police officer must undergo the same level of law enforcement training as a full-time paid officer, yet the reserve officer is a non-paid position.

Visitation Chaplains

Visitation chaplains (Lay Ministry Chaplains) typically volunteer their time meeting special needs at the county lockup, correctional facilities, assisted living facilities, hospitals, and so forth. While a full-time correctional chaplain will have to contend with the rigors of prison politics and life on the inside behind the walls, the visitation chaplain (volunteer) will only be tasked with providing the inmates with basic religious needs. Such as providing religious services, spiritual counseling, and performing ceremonial duties. In hospital-related ministries, the visitation chaplain will be tasked with visiting sick and dying patients and will report directly to the on-duty (senior) chaplain. In most cases, these types of ministerial duties are usually part of a church outreach ministry to meet the community's spiritual needs.

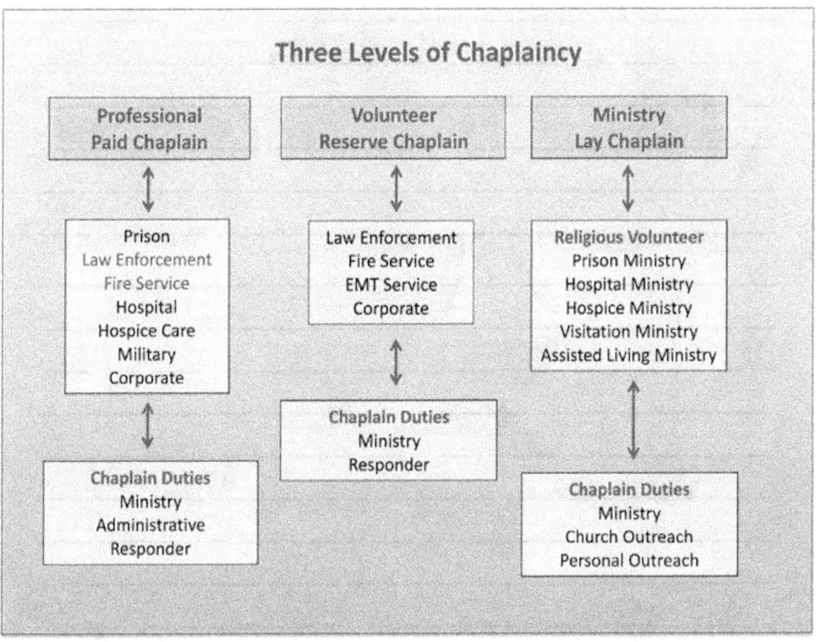
Three Levels of Chaplaincy
Professional
Paid Chaplain
Volunteer
Reserve Chaplain
Ministry
Lay Chaplain
Prison
Law Enforcement
Fire Service
Hospital
Hospice Care
Military
Corporate
Law Enforcement
Fire Service
EMT Service
Corporate
Religious Volunteer
Prison Ministry
Hospital Ministry
Hospice Ministry
Visitation Ministry
Assisted Living Ministry
Chaplain Duties
Ministry
Administrative
Responder
Chaplain Duties
Ministry
Responder
Chaplain Duties
Ministry
Church Outreach
Personal Outreach

Student Notes

Lesson 2

Chaplain and Volunteers

The Realities of Prison

> ***. . . I was in prison, and you came to me.***
>
> ***(Matthew 25:36)***

Often viewed as unredeemable and societal throwaways, thousands of people find themselves a guest of the state and federal prison system. It provides an excellent opportunity to reach people who have reached a low point in their lives and help them on their journey on the road back to redemption. While heeding the call of Christ, many Christian believers know very little about the prison system and the protocols that are in place that govern the interaction between the incarcerated and those who desire to introduce religious services to the inmate population. To be successful, you must possess a basic understanding of the rules of conduct, and to do so; you must learn something about the prison system. Let us examine the arrest process so that we may gain an understanding of the penal system.

When arrested, law enforcement will book the arrestee into custody at the county receiving facility. The jailer, detention officer, or deputy will take charge of the prisoner and begin the intake process. If any prisoner is combative, suicidal, or is a crucial witness to a crime, prisoners will be placed in segregated housing for their safety or the safety of others. Eventually, inmates are placed in a pretrial facility while awaiting a trial or final sentencing. The crime that land people in jail or prison are vast in number and maybe a simple as non-violent crimes such as check and credit card fraud to first-degree murder. The most common arrest is usually drug-related and involves criminal activities such as drug use, trafficking, distribution, and burglary. Predatory crimes such as child molestation, rape, and murder are part of the plethora of crimes that a chaplain must contend with from both a religious and security standpoint.

The newly incarcerated are sometimes in denial of their circumstances resulting in combative behavior. In the case of the suspect who is arrested for driving while under the influence (DUI), they may be too intoxicated to reason with or have an informative conversation. It is essential to be mindful of the security and informational risk when ministering to an inmate.

Suppose the inmate is involved in a current case that is under investigation. In that case, the chaplain must maintain absolute confidentiality in the matter to not impair evidence or witness testimony. In most cases, the inmate will be transferred to a Pretrial facility while awaiting trial unless there is a specific concern that prohibits the inmate from moving to a facility where the inmate may contact potential witnesses co-conspirators. In such cases, the inmate would be deemed a "keep-away" and remanded to another secure facility.

In the County Jail, inmate housing will differ depending on the inmate's security level and range from minimum security to maximum security. Some county jails classify their inmates using a color-coded wristband system to identify the inmate's security level and risk. An inmate wearing a blue band may indicate that the individual is a sexual predator or child molester in some facilities. In contrast, an orange band may designate the person as a danger to staff. Violent individuals will typically remain in handcuffs at all times during cell movement.

Maximum Security Inmates

Access to maximum-security inmates often comes with restrictions due to safety issues. In the State and Federal prison system, the security classification of inmates will determine the institution's level where an inmate will do his or her time of incarceration. Understanding the duties of a correctional chaplain will provide an atmosphere of safety in an otherwise dangerous environment.

Duties of a Correctional Chaplain

If you are serving as a paid chaplain for the Federal Bureau of Prisons (BOP), the scope of chaplaincy will far exceed that of your religious persuasion. While a BOP chaplain is required to perform the ordinances of their faith to the incarcerated of similar background, the chaplain will be asked to manage the needs of other religious groups. The chaplain is not required to perform services for those that are in different communities of beliefs. However, the chaplain will be needed to address the issues of religious diets, religious holidays, and religious supplies, perform death notifications as well as be available to meet the counseling need of the inmate population both religious and non-religious. Institutional chaplains are responsible for volunteer activities, volunteer training, maintaining chapel records, religious diets, having a working knowledge of the government database, and preparing the Religious Services Department for government audits.

State facilities often assign their chaplains duties within their faith group through their required duties and mandates may be similar to that of a federal chaplain. Volunteer chaplains have fewer restrictions and are primarily concerned with meeting the personal religious needs of the inmate as prescribed by their system of beliefs. If a county, detention facility or local jail does not have an on-duty chaplain available during a time of crisis, the volunteer chaplain may be asked to provide emergency services such as death notifications and crisis (Spiritual) counseling. In general, the volunteer chaplain

(Religious volunteer) will conduct religious services and work under the authority of the chaplain or volunteer coordinator.

Comparative Duties

FULL TIME CHAPLAIN DUTIES AND RESPONSIBILITY	VOLUNTEER CHAPLAIN DUTIES AND RESPONSIBILITY
Administrative • Correctional staff • Security staff • Associate Wardens • Warden • Training Department • Government audits	**Volunteerism** • Providing religious services • Counseling • Special Programs • Baptisms
Religious services • Provide religious programing • Coordinating religious groups • Baptisms • Counseling • Death Notifications • Crisis Intervention and more	**Chaplain/Volunteer Chaplain** Both serve an important role in ministry to the incarcerated and one cannot function without the other.

What you need to know about the Prison Rape Elimination Act

Whether you are a full time or volunteer chaplain, you will be required to receive four to six hours of orientation training before officiating religious services to the inmate population for the first time. Orientation will include instruction on the Prison Rape Elimination Act (PREA), entrance and exit procedures, inmate manipulation and con games, hostage situations, security protocols, and more. Volunteerism should never minimize institutional safety and security. As a volunteer, you will be exposed to institutional operations and will be expected to maintain the same level of security as any security or correctional staff member. Any concerns should be addressed to the on-duty chaplain or volunteer coordinator.

In 2003, during the George Bush presidency the U.S. Congress unanimously passed the Prison Rape Elimination Act as a result of the continued escalation of reported sexual assaults in the prison system. New legislation established a new set of protocols and mandatory reporting requirements to combat the increase of sexual assaults. While many institutions are playing catch-up establishing PREA protocols, most prison facilities have PREA protocols in place, require both staffs, and volunteer to be familiar with inmate victimization. More than likely, during the orientation process staff and volunteers, will receive instruction on the topic. As a chaplain or volunteer, the rules that regulate mandated reporting applies, and if an inmate approaches you regarding a violation, confidentiality cannot be offered.

Definition of Sexual Misconduct

Any behavior or act of a sexual nature, directed toward a person under the care, custody, or the supervision of the custodial institution regardless of the participants claim that the encounter is consensual is deemed as misconduct and a felony crime punishable by imprisonment. Percentagewise, based on the January 2011, Bureau of Justice Statistics, 65% of incarcerated males as victims of sexual assault, while only 35% of female inmates were victims of sexual assaults perpetrated by other inmates. It is estimated that inmates 47% between the ages of 18 & 25 will be assaulted while incarcerated. It is also estimated that 53% of White inmates will become victims of sexual assault as opposed to 35% Black inmates, and 11% Hispanic inmates. Only 5 to 10% of sexual abuses are reported by staff members; 27 % of reports are reported by their family members. Victims who have suffered from sexual abuse are:

- 3 times more likely to suffer from depression
- 4 times more likely to commit suicide
- 6 times more likely to suffer from PTSD
- 13 times more likely to abuse alcohol
- 26 times more likely to abuse drugs

WHO ARE THE VICTIMS AND WHO ARE THE PERPETRATORS?

The entertainment industry often portrays the topic of sex behind the prison walls in a comedic fashion and statements like *"The perp had it coming to him" or "When you get to prison Buba will have his way with you"* has been the conversation of many crimes show reruns. As officers, correctional staff, and religious volunteers, we are held to a higher standard of conduct and our personal feelings about corrections whatever they may be are not relevant. With prisons, detention centers, and pre-trial holding facilities having to endure endless annual PREA audits, minimizing PREA concerns is not an option for the correctional worker. The fact remains that the incarcerated have minimal freedoms and their day-to-day existence is governed by controlled movement, which is coordinated by security and correctional staff. There is no such thing as consensual sex while incarcerated, therefore any sexual act between inmates or between an inmate and staff member is viewed as a serious violation under the color of authority. In cases where there is staff, misconduct the inmate will always be seen as the victim and any staff violations felony that is accompanied with a sentence in a US prison facility. The following checklist will help separate those inmates who have the potential to become victims from those who are likely to be perpetrators.

Among Inmates who are the Victims?

- First-time, non-violent inmates
- Detained on a sexual offense against a minor
- Physically small or weak
- Traits viewed as effeminate
- Not streetwise
- Mental illness
- Disliked by other inmates/staff

Among Inmates who are the Perpetrator?

- Accustomed to prison life
- Previous incarceration or serving a long sentence
- Gang affiliated
- Persons who are accustomed to perpetrating acts of violence towards others.
- Physically strong
- Inmates who are non-compliant and who are likely to break prison rules

AGAIN, THERE IS NO SUCH THING AS SEXUAL CONSENT BETWEEN STAFF OR INMATES

It is the responsibility (It is the law) of all correctional staff and volunteers to take immediate action when sexual assaults are reported by the inmates. There is a Zero (0%) tolerance within the corrections, whether county, state or federal prisons of sexual abuse and sexual harassment. Sexual misconduct perpetrated by staff on an inmate is considered an abuse of power under the guise of authority. Again, all state and federal prisons and county jails have a "ZERO-TOLERANCE POLICY" and any sexual activities whether perpetrated by staff or inmate is punishable by imprisonment. Failure to Act and report misconduct could lead to criminal prosecution or civil damages. Most all correctional and detention facilities are continuing to update their PREA policy and provide ongoing training to their correctional staff.

Your duty to report sexual misconduct

The prison system requires all correctional staff and volunteers to report any, suspicion, or information regarding an allegation of sexual harassment or misconduct. (Mandatory Reporting Laws - Per PREA Standard 115.61) Correctional staff and volunteers are not required to validate whether or not a sexual assault has occurred, as a mandated reported all suspicious activities must be reported. If you are approached by an inmate who is claiming that he or she has been a victim of sexual abuse, some protocols must be carefully followed. First, ask the inmate what their full is name then ask if they have their prison identification card available. Most prisons issue their inmate's identification cards, which is used much like a credit card to purchase commissary items and to identify themselves to staff. Inmates are accustomed to being asked by staff for their IDs as part of their daily prison regiment and should be willing to provide it as a matter of habit. Preserve and protect any crime scene until the collection of evidence has taken place or you have been relieved by a superior staff member, and request that the victim does not take any actions that could destroy vital evidence. The following is the initial response protocol that should happen when a PREA incident has occurred.

Activate alarm if needed

Under the Good Samaritan Act, the average person may choose to render aid to a person who is in physical need but is not obligated to do so. However, as a correctional employee or volunteer serving in the penal system, you are considered a mandated reporter, and it is your responsibility and duty to take immediate action even if there is only a suspicion of a violation. A lack of response during a time of need may result in punitive action by the state. The following steps will better equip you to take proper action when the circumstances dictate.

- Take the alleged victim to a private, secure location, bag hands if possible. (Paper Bag)
- Contact Supervisor/inform
- Separate victim/suspect
- Secure crime scene
- Listen to victim, take notes
- Assess medical and custody needs
- Initiate time log (Inmate Victim PREA)
- Give time log to supervisor upon arrival.

Preservation of Evidence

It is important to make every effort to secure both the victim, and if possible, the suspect identity for legal purposes. It may be as simple as asking the victim if they are able to provide the identity of the perpetrator. If feasible, the victim should be detained by the staff member for his or her own safety until appropriate help arrives. Paying close attention to these steps will aid both security and medical staff in preserving of crucial boldly evidence that can be documented and later utilized in court. In the correctional system, all sexual encounters, whether it be staff on inmate or inmate on inmate, is viewed as a PREA violation. Even if the victim claims that the sexual act was consensual, or fabricates a story then later retracts the story, the inmate is still viewed as a victim of rape and is to be treated as such. The following set of protocols applies.

Do not allow the inmate to,

- Shower
- Wash Hands
- Brush Teeth or Rinse Mouth
- Remove Clothing Without Medical Supervision
- Use Restroom Facilities
- Consume Any Liquids

Dynamics of Sexual Abuse / Harassment in Confinement

The main dynamics, as experienced by inmates, are power, dominance and control. Common reactions to sexual assault are broken down into three categories.

1. Emotional responses
2. cognitive responses (knowledge or awareness)
3. Behavioral responses

Communicating With the Victim

When communicating with the victim be sincere without appearing to lay blame or make accusations particularly when dealing with the gay lesbian and transgender community. LGBT).

- Allow the victim to talk while you actively listen and take metal notes.
- Be sure to show verbal and non-verbal signs of interest in the discussion.
- Assure confidentiality but be clear that relevant information must be reported per federal policy.

A DIFFERENT WORLD - THE ANATOMY OF A SETUP

Since inmate manipulation of staff is a severe problem in the prison system, the chaplain and chaplain volunteer must be aware of their surroundings and be cautious of overly friendly inmate behavior. Some inmates may try to find some common ground with a staff member to establish a relationship, thus creating a portal for staff abuse. While the religious community enjoys more liberties than most correctional staff when it comes to inmate contact, care should be taken, and the chaplain and volunteer should always maintain a professional relationship with the inmate population to avoid the danger of inmate manipulation. The following is a set of guidelines that will help correctional workers determine if a staff member has been compromised.

The Model Inmate

Inmates can be like predators and chameleons, changing their demeanor, mood, and behavior to capture their prey. The model inmate is a skilled actor. Not all inmates fall into the category of a manipulator, and most are grateful for the care that is provided by the religious services department. However, there are those inmates who are willing to cross boundaries in order to accomplish their goal.

How to Prevent Boundary Violations

- ✓ Avoid identifying with inmates.
- ✓ Never place yourself in a situation where a sense of obligation exists.
- ✓ Use empathy instead of sympathy with inmates.

If you strictly adhere to the following principles, would-be manipulators will leave you alone. Most inmates will look to you as someone they can trust and emulate. Never do anything to, for, or with an inmate that you would be ashamed to share with your peers or supervisor. Keep everything out in the open. The following set of guidelines are designed to help you to evaluate how an inmate may view you as a person regardless of whether the representation is correct.

Guidelines for Self-Evaluation

- Am I overly friendly or familiar?
- Do I appear gullible?
- Do inmates consider me too trusting?
- Am I sympathetic?
- Is my demeanor timid?
- Is my enforcement of rules non-existent, or consistent?
- Do I share personal problems with inmates?
- Do I check the validity of inmate information?
- Do I let things slide, which should be addressed immediately?
- Do I have difficulty with command, control, or saying no?
- Do I circumvent minor rules?
- Do I allow the taking of liberties?
- Can I be made to feel obligated?
- Am I easily distracted?

Continued Guidelines for Self-Evaluation

Recognizing one is vulnerabilities does not mean that a person is unfit for a career in corrections. Neither does it mean you must change your personality. It does mean you need an alternative approach to your way of dealing with inmates. Stop the game before it begins.

- Most volunteers violate boundaries out of inexperience or ignorance.
- Most withdraw from the game because of a distinct feeling that "something is not quite right."
- For whatever reason, we realize what is going on before it is too late.

Contributing Factors

There are steps you can take to avoid becoming a victim of inmate manipulation. Knowing areas of risk and exposure will help you to avoid the dangers.

- Isolated posts, jobs, areas
- Learn the job from an inmate
- Staff must "pay their dues"
- We did it and succeeded, so should they!
- Friendliness and Over-Familiarization
- Appearance and Body Language
- Listening Observation
- Selection of a Victim – Intentional and Accidental
- Testing Staff/Rule Bending/Asking for Things
- Support System/We – They Syndrome
- Plea for Help
- Offer of Protection
- Allusions to Sex
- Touch System
- Rumor Mill

Are We Paying Attention to the Inmate?

- Over-identifying with inmates "My Inmate"
- Horseplay with inmates

- Inmates know personal staff information
- Inmates with letters/photos of staff
- Staff granting special requests or favors
- Inmates repeatedly in unauthorized areas
- Staff spending an unexplainable amount of time with inmates

Summary

Length of service, education, or experience has no direct bearing on victim selection. New employees are especially vulnerable due to a lack of understanding of their job and environment while experienced employees become vulnerable because they become complacent. It is essential to be vigilant of your surroundings and mindful of intuitional policies and procedures. Protocols may differ from state to state, from state to the Federal Bureau of Prisons as well as privatized prisons; however, the laws on PREA are universal in all counties, state, and federal facility.

Student Notes

Lesson 3

Duties of the Emergency Service Chaplain

During times of crisis, as a chaplain, you may be asked to minister to people who are going through different types of emotional trauma. In the role of a chaplain, you are considered a caregiver as well as a spiritual advisor. However, unless you are also licensed as a professional clinician, you must remain in your field of expertise. In general, chaplains are ministers, not therapists, and even though what we provide as responders can be very therapeutic, most chaplains are not qualified to diagnose and treat medically related emotional issues. For the well-meaning chaplain, this can spiral into a legal quagmire that can result in both civil and criminal liabilities depending on the circumstances surrounding the incident if caution is ignored.

Agency Confidentiality

Most chaplains will be exposed to confidential information that is not for public consumption. More than likely, the official agency will have a policy handbook, and the chaplain will be required to sign a confidentiality document restricting the distribution of departmental information. Confidential information is not to be shared with social media, news media, or the public. Most public agencies have a Public Relations Officer (PRO) who is assigned to update media and the public during newsworthy events. Never speak to the media unless you authorized or commanded to do so by your commanding officer or supervisor.

A Ministry of Presence

As clergy entering the field of chaplaincy, we bring with us our religious concepts and ideologies. Religion and denominational debates can do significant harm and destroy an established chaplain program undoing years of hard work and relationship building with departmental personnel. Often inexperienced chaplains enter the world of chaplaincy with the mindset of the church pastor and expect the same outcome when communicating with emergency service personnel that would be customary in a church setting. Protocols within the emergency services communities are much different from what is found within the walls of the local church. Most agencies frown on proselytization unless invited to do so by personnel. In most cases, if proselytizing becomes an ongoing issue within the agency setting, the chaplain may be asked to resign his commission. The chaplaincy is a ministry of presence and is not a platform for recruitment to fill empty pews. Many people you meet may have different religious persuasions, and the opportunity for evangelism may be non-existent. As a ministry of presence, Christ is demonstrated in our actions more so than public evangelism.

Providing Comfort during Crisis and Trauma

Shootings, suicides, and traffic accidents are frequent particularly in larger metropolitan areas where there is a higher probability that such events will occur. Hospital and hospice care chaplaincy though not as graphic as other types of service, still exposes the chaplain to those individuals who are sick and dying. When responding to a call for service, you will encounter many emotions. During times of tragedy, emergency service personnel are responsible for dealing with the matter at hand and often are unavailable to address those who are in crisis. The victims perceive an adverse reaction by law enforcement officials as harsh and uncaring.

Law enforcement when responding to the suicide, mainly if the suicide is a self-inflicted gunshot wound requires that the event and venue be treated as a crime scene even though there may be no evidence of an actual crime. In most cases, protocol requires that before a family can take possession of the body after a horrific event, the coroner's office must determine that no foul play has taken place. For family members, this can cause additional stress and anger towards emergency service workers.

During this time, the chaplain can serve as a liaisón between emergency services and the victim's family, providing updates and information when it is permissible. In many situations, victims may express anger towards the chaplain because of what they represent. Anger towards God is a temporary coping mechanism during times of tragedy. Such attacks should not be taken personally, as each victim may respond differently to traumatic events.

The following is a list of emergency callouts that are most common in emergency services chaplaincy.

Officer-Involved Shootings

When an officer is involved in a shooting incident, in most cases, the officer is placed on paid administrative leave. The officer is required to have limited contact with the general public, including family until a review committee or the Office of Internal Affairs have the opportunity to debrief the officer and clear the officer of any wrongdoing. Such events are often an emotional time for the officer. The chaplain may be allowed to spend time with the officer and provide emotional support during this time of crisis. Most likely, the chaplain will be a member of the department, allowing the chaplain conditional access to the officer under review. Despite recent media coverage of law enforcement involved shootings, it is an emotional and traumatic time for the officer.

In the Line of Duty Death

In the line of duty, death is one of the more stressful times for law enforcement and fire agencies. In addition to an already stressful work environment, the loss of a fellow officer or firefighter is not only traumatic for fellow responders and employees but the family of the fallen personnel as well. Your duties as an emergency services chaplain may include accompanying departmental command staff to the home of the officer and notifying the family of the death. Chaplains spend countless hours ministering to employees and are often involved in funeral perpetrations. Agencies, in larger cities, there are usually teams of chaplains within the department who will assist the lead chaplain with agency needs.

Visit Sick or Injured Department Employees

Chaplains are often called upon to minister to personnel who are injured on the job or who are facing a sudden illness. Ministry outreach includes ministering to the families of emergency services staff and departmental employees who have retired.

Callouts and Warbags

Public service agencies rely upon chaplains to respond to emergency callouts. Larger cities who commission a large number of chaplain volunteers will usually have a callout system in place where a particular chaplain is assigned a timeslot and is on-call to respond on a moment's notice to emergencies. Some agencies use a paging system or assign a department cell phone used for emergency purposes only. When responding to an emergency, chaplains should have ready a "War-Bag" with all the essential items necessary to render assistance. A "War-Bag" is usually a black duffel bag that contains items that are used in the performance of your duties such as a high-quality flashlight, communion supplies if allowed, a notepad for taking notes and writing reports. Your wardrobe supplies should include a ball cap and extra polo shirt and a windbreaker with the designation of a chaplain on the front and backside of the jacket, rubber gloves, and emergency resource handout material. You may want to include in your arsenal of supplies items for children such as a small stuffed animal, coloring books crayons, and games.

Other Major Incidents Include but not limited to,

- Suicides / Suicide attempts
- Drowning accidents
- SIDS death (Children)
- Death by natural causes (Old age and nursing homes)

Crisis Intervention

Chaplains are taking a more active role within law enforcement agencies, fire services, hospitals, and prisons serving as members of their in-house Crisis Support Team. They work with the Mental Health community conducting Critical Incident Stress Debriefings for first responders after significant events as well as provide aftercare. A significant event includes natural disasters, in the line of duty death, aircraft, train, and major car accidents, just to name a few.

Notifying next-of-kin in the event of death or serious injury incidents

Performing notifications are covered in greater detail in Lesson 5 of this training program and include,

- Notifications to the families of emergency services personnel
- Notifications to the general public (Death or accident)
- Notifications to the incarcerated (Prison inmates)
- Hospital notifications

Victim Assistance

It is beneficial for a chaplain to develop a working relationship with local agencies for referrals and resources. The chaplain should have available resources that can be handed out after a significant incident where there are victims such as domestic violence, funeral resources, and public assistance materials. Local law enforcement agencies, county mental health, mortuaries, the Coroner's Office, local hospitals, the Red Cross, and courthouses may be able to provide victim assistance handout material free of charge. You may be asked to do a follow-up and offer support for victims who are in crisis as well as provide additional counseling for families or individuals who are experiencing stress after an event. Support is typically done temporarily until additional family, local clergy, or other resources are made available.

Care and Compassion

- Provide confidentiality and counsel to emergency service personnel
- To be available to families of officers during times of stress and emotional trauma
- Provide personal or family counseling

Spiritual Guidance and Care

Chaplaincy is often demonstrated by action rather than by words, and respect cannot be demanded, it must be earned. Earning and gaining the respect of emergency service officials is necessary to be efficient and have credibility as a chaplain. However, it is essential to be mindful of the religious and spiritual needs of the emergency service worker and recommend them to their clergy when necessary. At times, it may seem that some emergency service personnel have no religious affiliation, never assume that their spiritual needs are not being met elsewhere. Emergency service workers have lives outside of their day-to-day work life, and many participate in local worship services in their community. In contrast, in the prison system due to their circumstances, and limited choices, the incarcerated rely heavily on the chaplain and religious volunteers for their religious and spiritual needs and do so until their release date. However, public service chaplaincy has different protocols and expectations, and as a chaplain, you should be familiar with what they are and meet those needs accordingly.

Special Events

Perform invocations and benedictions at department functions such as,

- Promotion and award ceremonies
- Building and facility dedications
- Media events and inaugurations ceremonies
- Department academy graduations
- Preside at weddings/funerals

Regardless of the opportunities that may be provided you as a chaplain, it is imperative to remember that you are a guest in someone's backyard and agency protocols will always prevail when a need arises.

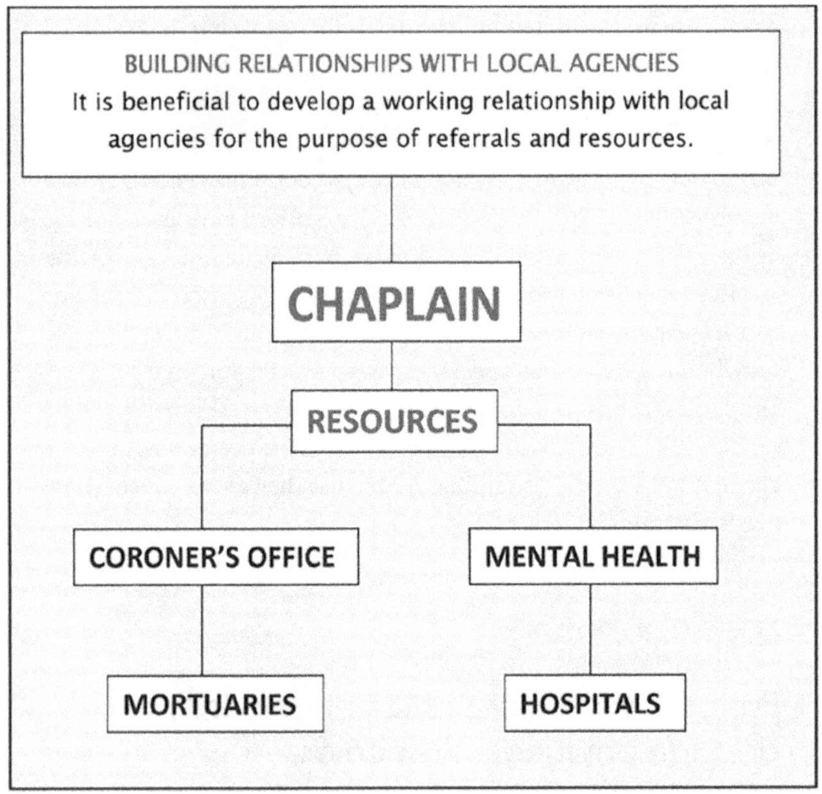

Student Notes

Part 2

Understanding Protocol and Ethics

Lesson 4

Chaplains and Emergency Protocols and Procedures

Command Structure - Perhaps the most significant failure among individuals who serve as institutional chaplains is that they forget the cardinal rule. Once the chaplain leaves the walls of his church and enters the world of institutional chaplaincy, they are a guest of the institution, and they can be replaced if departmental protocols are breached. Generally, there is a command structure in place be it in law enforcement, fire services or hospitals. It is accompanied by rules and regulations which the chaplain must adhere to if they are to achieve any amount of success among those they serve. In every law enforcement agency, emergency response organization, hospital and prison facility, there is a chain of command. Many chaplains have been relieved of their duties as a result of conflict with command staff or their insistent interference with departmental and institutional protocols as well as regulatory violations. A strong desire to minister the Gospel message often clouds the judgment of the chaplain because they approach the ministry from a church standpoint rather than an industry standpoint, forgetting that the chaplain serves at the pleasure of the agency or institution. Most professional chaplains will be required to undergo orientation and training so that they become familiar with agency rules.

Emergency Call Outs

A chaplain may be called to respond to a major tragedy such as a suicide, child drowning, traffic collision, or a community disaster. Emergency callouts will depend upon victim needs and the needs of emergency personnel. When arriving at the emergency scene, it is incumbent upon the chaplain to determine who is in charge. This person is generally referred to as the on-scene commander who will provide further instructions. There may be aspects of the emergency that cannot be made public to the family until the conclusion of the investigation. The chaplain must also be mindful that the emergency may have been deemed a crime scene and because of the collecting of evidence by crime scene technicians, the chaplain's ability to move about the crime scene may be restricted.

Providing information

One of the more challenging aspects of a tragedy is the limited amounts of information that can be shared with the survivors. While specific information may not be available to share with the survivors, the appearance that efforts are being made to keep the family informed will often defuse an otherwise hostile situation. When communicating with the victim's family, you may want to use the following statements.

> *"I have spoken with the person in charge, and they have assured me that when more information becomes available, I can pass on the information to you and the rest of the family. In the meantime, I will be with you every step of the way."*

> *"I know this must be very frustrating for you. When I hear anything further, I promise I will let you know."*

Incident Command Protocols

In the event of a major disaster such as earthquakes, tornados, fire, and floods, Incident Command Protocols are generally utilized by federal, state and local governments. Once Incident Command protocols have been initiated, local law enforcement, fire service, hospitals, and EMS will activate emergency personnel. Local detentions and prisons facilities will go on lockdown until further notice. If the incident is primarily fire-related, fire services will assume command and all other agencies will follow their emergency protocols and directives.

Prison Riots

In the event of a prison riot, prison officials will assume command of the situation and outside agencies will follow their lead since prison officials have a better understanding of their environment and internal dangers. Overall, the circumstances of the disaster will determine the chain of command. During disasters, police, fire services, and EMS will coordinate their efforts with local hospitals in order to prepare and care for the injured. Chaplains from all branches of government, hospitals and private organizations will likely be assigned to care for grieving families and aid in emergency relief.

Arriving on the scene of a Traffic Accident

When stopping to offer assistance to first responders during a traffic accident, there are some basic rules to follow, which will not only help the chaplain gain respect but also demonstrate professionalism. The chaplain must be cautious of his or her immediate surroundings and must be confident that the area in question is safe to approach. For example, an oil tanker truck rollover may present hazmat issues that make it a hazardous proposition. Deadly fumes and spillage from the rollover tanker may create hazards for personnel who do not have the benefit of protective wear, and any attempt to approach the victim will only create more danger for first responders and the chaplain. Another area of concern is traffic safety when exiting the vehicle when there are traffic conditions. The chaplain must exercise extreme caution when first approaching emergency services personnel. The chaplain should be direct and to the point.

Communicating the right way:

> *"My name is Chaplain Smith with Chaplains International (or your agency) do you need assistance?"*

Generally, law enforcement and fire officials tend to be uncomfortable when random individuals are approaching the scene of a traffic accident. Taking the direct approach by identifying yourself as a chaplain and stating your business will help to alleviate tensions and concerns that first responders may have regarding your involvement.

Ride-Along

Most law enforcement or fire agencies have minimum requirements for service, and the requirements will vary from agency to agency. In some cases, public agencies will mandate that a reserve chaplain reside within fifty miles of the department or division they serve in order to respond promptly to emergency callouts. Rollcall or briefings usually precedes each shift and establishes daily routines and activities. During briefings, the watch sergeant will assign the officer his or her patrol vehicle and duty partner. If an officer is assigned to be a one-man unit, an area partner (second officer) will be assigned as a backup for traffic stops and calls for service.

Chaplains are assigned to ride with officers during their shift in order to get to know the officer and develop a clerical relationship.

While on patrol during a ride-along safety is paramount, and officer directives must be always followed. Chaplains who lack field experience are often seen as a liability, which poses additional concerns for the officer who is now responsible for the safety of the chaplain. Being familiar with departmental protocols will alleviate officer concerns and develop officer confidence in the chaplain's ability to perform his or her duties while under stressful conditions. During the patrol, there are times when officers will allow the chaplain to accompany them on a call for service, however, some officers may prefer that the chaplain remain in the patrol vehicle as a safety precaution.

Radio Traffic

The chaplain should become familiar with radio traffic and radio codes in the event of an emergency and the chaplain must call for help. If the chaplain is unfamiliar with emergency services, radio codes, then plain language should be used when communicating with the dispatcher. The dispatcher will want to know the following information:

1. Vehicle number (I.e., Shop# 155)
2. Your exact location (Address, street, and cross street)
3. Information about the Incident
4. Location and condition of the officer
5. The situation and hazards
6. Number of individuals involved

It is important to remember that when using the radio microphone, to press the talk button then release the button so the dispatcher or other officers can respond to your call. Your radio traffic must be direct and to the point since time is of the essence during a life-or-death situation. For example,

- *"Chaplain 7 (or vehicle number) to dispatch, officer down, officer needs assistance. Location 137 Center Lane, cross street, Center Lane and Vine!"*
- *"Chaplain 7 to dispatch, shots fired officer needs help. Location, 635 Sycamore Ave. Cross Street, Sycamore and Redwood Ave!"*
- *"Chaplain 7 to dispatch, 415 fight officer needs assistance or the officer is fighting with a combative suspect and needs help." Location, 635 Sycamore Ave. Cross Street, Sycamore and Redwood Ave!"*

Chaplain safety 101 is to always know your location and if possible, the nearest cross street so that responding officers can locate you in the event of a dangerous situation. Following these basic but essential protocols may save the life of the officer as well as the life of the chaplain.

Student Notes

Lesson 5

Pastoral Confidentiality and Ethics

In recent years, there has been an increasing number of lawsuits filed against clergy for the invasion of privacy, arising out of the disclosure of confidential information acquired during counseling sessions with parishioners. The result of these lawsuits has brought about more scrutiny when it comes to confidentiality and the release of personal information.[9]

Breach of Confidentiality - Case History

The case history of *Lightman v. Flaum* is one example of a violation of the clergy confidentially guidelines and sets a precedent for future lawsuits. In this case, the female plaintiff confided in two rabbis from the local Synagogue where she attended service. In her statement to the rabbis, she confessed that she was having an extramarital affair with another member of the congregation. Since the act of infidelity is a violation of rabbinical law, the two rabbis felt it necessary to breach confidentiality and report the conversation and the admission of infidelity to the parishioner's husband, which created additional stress on the already failing marriage. Deemed a breach of confidentiality, the parishioner filed a lawsuit against the two rabbis for violating clergy-penitent privileges. The two rabbis who were listed as defendants in the case argued that the filing was bogus based on their perceived obligation as rabbinical leaders to report such matters to other parishioners when deemed necessary and therefore petitioned the court for a dismissal of the complaint. The rabbis continued to argue the case stating that under the Religious Freedom Act, they were allowed the liberty to report any indiscretion to the plaintiff's husband if warranted. The trial court rejected the defendant's petition for a dismissal of the Plaintiff's complaint allowing for the continuation of the lawsuit.

Mandated Reporter vs. Confidentiality

There are other areas of concern that the counselor should be aware of and includes understanding the laws governing Mandated Reporting. Whether you are serving as a police officer, emergency services responder, prison worker, clergy, hospital staff, or a schoolteacher, Mandated Reporting regulations apply, and confidentiality is not a privilege.

One example, where clergy confidentiality privileges are non-applicable is in the matter about parent-child relationships. By 1974, all fifty states had mandatory reporting laws often referred to as "Child Protection Statutes." A crime perpetrated against minors, offer no clergy confidentiality privileges or protection from reporting a crime. Children are considered to have no voice thus are unable to defend or represent themselves as adults. It becomes the responsibility of the counselor, Christian Education Director, children minister, and youth counselor to report any crime, suspected or otherwise. Other clergy-penitent concerns involve confessions where the individual openly admits the intent to commit a crime, suicide, or an act of violence. By law, clergy (Mandated Reporter) are required to report any individual who has expressed the intent to commit a criminal act particularly when it involves violence. If while counseling an individual, it has been determined that the counselee intends to commit suicide, the counselor is obligated as a mandated reporter to report the threat. In general, the court system would prefer not to rely on testimony obtained by clergy while under the guise of confidentiality. However, the courts can make an official mandate requiring the counselor to reveal sensitive information if they deem it legally necessary.

What is Ethics?

Ethics is the discipline, which guides our judgment concerning the morality of human acts. The discipline of ethics employs the power of human reason, and all persons are bound in conscience to apply its principles to their conduct. Thus, ethics is a moral discipline dealing with human acts. Human acts are those actions performed by human beings, using their superior faculties of intellect and freewill, as opposed to those acts, which are common in the animal kingdom. Ethics is a discipline that studies the moral correctness of human behavior about our natural end. In summary, ethics is a science, which guides our judgment concerning morality. "Morals" is human conduct in the light of principles. A person can have good ethical concepts and bad morals, as in the case of someone who knows the principles but fails to apply them in concrete situations. Ethics is also called "moral philosophy."

It is distinct from "moral theology" although they bare a close relationship with each other. Ethics is based on human reason alone, which looks only to a natural end, while moral theology (Christian ethics) relies on faith as well as reason and recognizes a "supernatural end." Secular ethics/moral philosophy and Christian ethics/moral theology both deal with human acts. The formal object of moral theology, however, is the morality of human actions towards a "supernatural end." As God is in control, we cannot choose a natural end but must strive to a supernatural end (according to God's will).

Gratuity and Favors

Areas of ethical concern include the conduct of the chaplain on and off duty. As clergy, society tends to hold the minister to a higher standard, and there are regulatory rules regarding ethics within a departmental setting. Regulations concerning favors, gifts, and gratuities received by department personnel are frowned upon by law enforcement and fire agencies. In many instances, a chaplain in uniform walks into a coffee shop and is offered a free meal or a substantial discount because of his emergency services affiliation. While the owner can provide the chaplain a free meal or discount as an act of kindness in recognition of his contribution to the community, the respective agency may view it as a gratuity in return for favors.

Chaplain Badge and Uniform

Many police and fire agencies issue official badges to their commissioned chaplains for the purpose of establishing quick and visible identification during times of crisis. In most cases, municipal and county agencies will issue a traditional metal badge, usually identical to the standard police officer badge with one exception. Where the official title of police officer or officer rank is customarily found, usually on the upper panel of the shield, the police officer title reads chaplain or police chaplain. Some agencies will only issue their chaplains cloth badges while others do not include a badge as part of their uniform code. Many chaplains as an option carry a generic chaplain's badge (Non-affiliation) along with their official department issued pocket identification card. If dressed in traditional class A or class C uniforms, the chaplain will most likely wear a badge on the left breast portion of the uniform provided that it is uniform policy compliant. If placed on call by a public service agency, the chaplain may be permitted to respond to a callout wearing a black or green raid jacket with a back panel attached with the title of chaplain across the back portion of the jacket. Provided that permission has been granted by the agency they serve, the chaplain while on duty may display a chaplain's badge at belt level for identification purposes.

Many agencies prefer the chaplain to carry an organizational shield instead of a public agency shield, thus representing their organizational affiliation rather than the agency of service. Whether a commissioned chaplain is issued an agency shield or carries a badge issued by their chaplain's organization, there are rules of conduct that must be followed at all times. A person who misrepresents themselves as something other than a chaplain in or out of uniform and does so wearing a badge is in serious violation of the law, and it is considered a breach of ethics. This type of scrutiny of ethical conduct holds true among law enforcement and fire agencies. Most chaplain badges are designed using the same dye-cast mold as badges used by public service agencies and can easily be misidentified as a police officer or firefighter shield. Impersonating a police officer or fire fighter is deemed a serious violation of the law and is punishable by both a fine and jail time. Chaplain badges are designed to be a tool for quick identification during a crisis and other major events and should not be used for the purpose of receiving favors.

The Ten Commandments lists the major violations of natural moral laws that address:

- ✓ The existence of God
- ✓ The worship of God
- ✓ Obligation to those in authority over us (God and parents)
- ✓ Sanctity of life
- ✓ Sanctity of marriage
- ✓ Conducts in living with others: (respecting the properties of others)

The Natural Moral Law is not meant to interfere with our liberty but guide us in the proper use of our freedom. The Ten Commandments are a set of God's directions on how we can avoid harm to ourselves and attain happiness both in this life and in the life to come.

Student Notes

Part 3

Responding to Emergency Call-Outs

Lesson 6

Dealing with Suicidal People

Responding to Suicide Call Outs and on Scene Protocols

Estimates by the World Health Organization states that approximately 1 million people die each year from suicide. Suicide is a permanent reaction to a temporary problem, and any suicidal statements or attempts must be taken seriously. Say an individual confides in you and states he feels suicidal, you should do everything within your field of expertise to help that individual, including advising him/her to seek professional help immediately.

The Jumper or Man with a Gun

When approaching someone who is attempting suicide, the chaplain must approach with caution. Someone who is adamant about committing suicide can pose a danger to the chaplain as well as the emergency responder. If the person sees the responder as a threat, he or she may react negatively. A person with a gun may instinctively turn the gun on the chaplain or the responder then take his own life. When approaching the subject, it is essential to remain calm and avoid excessive body movement, such as the use of your hands while communicating with the subject. The subject may feel that you are approaching him with the intent of preventing him from committing the act of suicide and may react accordingly and complete the act. For example, a bridge jumper who has placed himself on the opposite side of the safety barrier may go through with the act of suicide if the person feels your motive is to apprehend him and prevent the action.

A person who is holding a gun to someone's head or is standing on the edge of a rooftop and threatens to jump, is in full command of the situation. Many times, a suicidal individual may feel they have gone too far and must go through with the act. The person may fear the possibility of incarceration, being held on a 72-hour hold as well as a loss of career and reputation. Do not deceive them but reinforce the idea that nothing has occurred that cannot be undone. The most powerful tool you have as a responder is communication.

Attempted Suicide - Do's & Don'ts

When communicating with someone who is suicidal, be mindful of your body language. Your body language can convey a message, either positive or negative. For example, if you were to express your love for another person while shouting and shaking your fists, would the person view the gesture as positive or negative? Likely, from the person's perspective, the expression of love is overshadowed by the perception of contention and malice. The same is true when communicating with someone in a crisis. When approaching the subject, it is crucial to remain calm and avoid excessive body movement, such as the use of your hands. If possible, get the person to mirror you. Mirroring is a process of calmly and emotionally connecting with a person in crisis and getting them to pattern your behavior. Let us say a person is highly agitated and is experiencing anxiety. If your behavior is calm and peaceful, the person may unknowingly mirror your behavior. You may see a significant change in the person's breathing, posture, and speech patterns. The idea is to defuse the crisis and to help the person see that there are other options.

Zone of Safety

When responding to a suicidal person, the responder must maintain a certain distance from the individual to prevent the possibility of becoming a casualty of the crisis. As a responder, you should never be so close to the person that they can grab hold of you, causing you bodily harm. The distance between you and the person is significant when confronting a suicidal subject with a knife. If a police officer is confronted by someone with a screwdriver, in many cases, the officer will shoot the suspect in self-defense. While a screwdriver may appear to be a less-lethal weapon, it can be quickly plunged into the victim and cause blunt trauma as well as death. If something as simple as a screwdriver can cause great concern to the responder, then a person with a sharp object such as a knife should be handled with great care. In this scenario, the person may be holding the blade to their throat or in the case of a hostage situation, to the neck of the hostage. An individual attempting suicide with a firearm is going to be far more challenging to deal with because there is no safe distance by which you can position yourself other than taking cover behind a safety barrier. Approaching a suicidal person with a weapon is usually going to be at the discretion of the responding agency. Other emergency personnel may be charged with the task of apprehending the individual to take control of the situation. However, it is not likely that you, as a chaplain, will be asked to assist. Therefore, your role is a ministry of communication, compassion, and presence.

COMMON MISCONCEPTIONS ABOUT SUICIDE

When it comes to the topic of suicide, people have many misconceptions about the subject. As a chaplain and first responder, it is important to have a basic understanding of the topic in order to avoid mistakes that could potentially cause more harm. For example, while a person may experience emotional pain and suffering as a result of grief, or perhaps has a history of depression, emotional pain is not necessarily a sign of mental illness. Nonetheless, the talk of suicide should be viewed as a warning sign and taken seriously. Usually there are significant warning signs for suicide such as the person deep obsession about death and dying or openly talking about killing oneself. These are just a few of the warning signs to be on the lookout for and should be dealt with as soon as possible. A more subtle but equally dangerous warning sign of suicide is the person's sense of hopelessness accompanied by depression. Some experts suggest that ongoing feelings of hopelessness are a strong predictor of suicidal tendencies. People who feel hopeless may talk about "unbearable" feelings, predict a bleak future, and state that they have no future. To dispel some of the notions surrounding suicide the following question and answer quiz will help to address those concerns

Quick Quiz

People who talk about suicide will not really do it.
FALSE
Answer: *Almost everyone who commits or attempts suicide has given some clue or warning!*

Do not ignore suicide threats. Statements like *"you'll be sorry when I'm dead," "I can't see any way out,"* — no matter how casually or jokingly said, may indicate serious suicidal feelings.

Anyone who tries to kill him/herself must be crazy.
FALSE
Answer: *Most suicidal people are not psychotic or insane*

If a person is determined to kill him/her, nothing is going to stop them. **TRUE & FALSE**
Answer: Even the most severely depressed person has mixed feelings about death, wavering until the very last moment between wanting to live and wanting to die. ***Most suicidal people do not want death; they want***

the pain to stop. The impulse to end it all, however overpowering, does not last forever.

Talking about suicide may give someone the idea.
FALSE
Answer: You do not give a suicidal person morbid idea by talking about suicide

The opposite is true bringing up the subject of suicide and discussing it openly is one of the most helpful things you can do.
Source: SAVE – Suicide Awareness Voices of Education

SUICIDE PREVENTION STARTS BY ASKING KEY QUESTIONS

If you suspect that, someone is contemplating suicide or is expressing suicidal thoughts, being direct and asking questions will help to determine the level of threat. Dialog and asking open-ended questions will provide insight to the person's state of mind and provide an opportunity to defuse the situation and seek appropriate help.

1. *How are you coping with what has been happening in your life?*
2. *Do you ever feel like just giving up?*
3. *Are you thinking about dying?*
4. *Are you thinking about hurting yourself?*
5. *Are you thinking about suicide?*
6. *Have you ever thought about suicide before, or tried to harm yourself before?*
7. *Have you thought about how or when you will do it?*
8. *Do you have access to weapons or things that can be used as weapons to harm yourself?*

ADDITIONAL WARNING SIGNS

You cannot always tell when a loved one or friend is contemplating suicide. However, there are some telltale signs that can help identify a person who exhibiting suicidal behavior.

- ***Talking about suicide*** *— for example, making statements such as "I'm going to kill myself," "I wish I were dead" or "I wish I hadn't been born"*
- ***Getting the means to take your own life****, such as buying a gun or stockpiling pills*
- ***Withdrawing from social contact*** *and wanting to be left alone*
- ***Having mood swings****, such as being emotionally high one day and deeply discouraged the next*
- ***Being preoccupied with death****, dying or violence*
- ***Feeling trapped or hopeless*** *about a situation*
- ***Increasing use of alcohol*** *or drugs*
- ***Changing normal routine****, including eating, or sleeping patterns*
- ***Doing risky or self-destructive things****, such as using drugs or driving recklessly*
- ***Giving away belongings*** *or getting affairs in order when there is no other logical explanation for doing this*
- ***Saying goodbye to people*** *as if they won't be seen again*
- ***Developing personality changes*** *or being severely anxious or agitated, particularly when experiencing some of the warning signs listed above - (By Mayo Clinic Staff)*

HOW TO HANDLE A CONVERSATION OR PHONE CALL WITH A SUICIDAL PERSON

(By: David L. Conroy, PhD.)

1. ***Listen, no matter how negative the conversation*** *may seem. The fact that it exists is a positive sign, a cry for help.*
2. ***Be sympathetic, non-judgmental, patient, calm, accepting.*** *The caller has done the right thing by getting in touch with another person.*
3. ***If the person says, I am very depressed, I cannot go on, ask the question:*** *"Are you having thoughts of suicide?"*
4. ***If the answer is yes, you can ask additional questions:***

    a. *Have you thought about how you would do it? (PLAN)*
    b. *Do you have what you need? (MEANS)*
    c. *Have you thought about when you would do it? (TIME SET)*

Simply talking about their problems for a length of time with suicidal people will often help defuse the situation. **Ask if the person has taken any drugs or alcohol**, including prescription medication. If possible, get specific details. The most important pain-coping resource is the help of a trained mental health professional. A person who feels suicidal should get help and get it sooner rather than later.

RECAP - SUICIDE WARNING SIGNS

Talking about suicide

Any talk about suicide, dying, or self-harm, such as:

- *"I wish I hadn't been born"*
- *"If I see you again..."*
- *"I'd be better off dead."*

Seeking out lethal means

Seeking access to dangerous objects that could be used in a suicide attempt such as:

- *Knives / Guns / Pills*
- *Preoccupation with death*
- *Unusual focus on death, dying, or violence*
- *Writing poems or stories about death*
- *No hope for the future*
- *Feelings of helplessness and hopelessness*
- *There is no way out and things will never get better or change*
- *Self-loathing, self-hatred*
- *Feelings of worthlessness*
- *Guilt, shame, and self-hatred*
- *Feeling like a burden, ("Everyone would be better off without me")*
- *Getting affairs in order*
- *Making out a will and giving away prized possessions.*
- *Withdrawing from friends and family*
- *Self-destructive behavior*
- *Increased alcohol or drug use and reckless behavior*
- *A sudden sense of calm and happiness after being extremely depressed can mean that the person has planned to commit suicide.*

When someone becomes suicidal, the person develops tunnel vision with their full attention and focus on the matter before them. Overwhelmed by emotional stress, there is a strong sense that there is no possible outcome, but one. So, by identifying unusual or extreme behavior in someone who is otherwise calm and cognitive in his or her thought process could be what prevents a fatal outcome.

Resource

American Association of Suicidology
4201 Connecticut Ave. NW Suite 408
Washington, DC 20008
Phone: (202) 237-2280
Fax: (202 237-2282
Web: http://www.suicidology.org

Student Notes

Lesson 7

Basic Death Notification Procedures

In Person - Performing a death notification may seem to some to be a simple concept, one with minimal consequences. However, such perceptions are dangerous and can do a great deal of emotional harm if performed incorrectly. There are basic rules of engagement, and if done correctly, the person being notified may recall the notification in the future as kind and compassionate. **Therefore, adhering to a strong set of protocols will help to create a positive experience during moments of hardship and tragedy.**

If possible, it is always best to perform death notifications in person, not by telephone. There may be mitigating circumstances where that may be the only option however it is best to arrange for the death notification to be made in person, even if the survivor lives far away. If a notification is to be made in another city or state, it may be possible to reach out to local law enforcement, the medical examiner's office, or the Red Cross for additional assistance.

Time and Certainty - Timing and correct information is a crucial component when performing a notification. It is recommended that all notifications be performed within a 24-hour time period particularly if the death of the individual is a newsworthy event. The following are some basic rules that will help the notification process go smoothly.

- ✓ Provide notification as soon as possible
- ✓ Obtain positive identification of the deceased
- ✓ Notify next of kin and others living in the same household, including roommates and unmarried partners.
- ✓ Make sure that the information is accurate before conducting a notification as this will reduce the chance of unnecessary trauma.
- ✓ Gather detailed information, regarding the circumstances surrounding the death

If Possible, Do Notifications in Pairs

Always try to have two people present to make the death notification. Some notifications are sometimes accompanied by additional drama creating an unstable environment. Performing a notification in pairs provides a measure of safety and is beneficial especially when there are mutable victims involved. In the case of law enforcement involved notifications, the chaplain is usually accompanied by an officer.[10] In most cases upon completion of the notification, both the chaplain and office will the scene at the same time. However, in situations where the chaplain may be approached and ask to provide pastoral aftercare, it is recommended taking two separate vehicles. Finally, if there is more than one chaplain involved in the notification process then the team should decide who will take the lead as the primary responder and who will perform the actual notification[11]

Use Plain Language

Good communication, accurate information and having a presentation protocol in place are crucial when performing a death notification. Personal and environmental safety is extremely important for both the presenter and the victim. Since people are emotionally diverse, when it comes to receiving bad news and people can react differently to the announcement of the death of a loved one.

Sample of a proper notification

> *"My name is Chaplain Dale Scadron, and this is Chaplain Andrew Smith, and we represent the Glendale Police Department." Is your name Rebecca Chambers"* If the person answers yes then ask the following question? *"Is your husband Robert Chambers?"*

By this time the person is aware that there is a problem and may become agitated which is a normal response when receiving uncertain news.

> *"I have important information I would like to share with you but before we do may we come in and sit down?"*

It is best, if at all possible, to have the recipient (s) sit down before giving the notification for many different reasons. The recipient may be an elderly person who is prone to falling or perhaps a person who has a history of heart disease and may become unsteady during the notification process. By having the individual (s) sit down during the notification reduces the danger of the person potentially collapsing and incurring physical injuries due to the emotional shock.

> *"Is there anyone here in the home with you?"*

If there are additional people in the home, it is recommended that you tell the recipient that you would like for those people to be present during the notification. If there are children in the home, you may want to ask if one of the adults can take the children into another room. Often, the parents may prefer to notify the children separately. Once the home environment is staged, the notification can begin.

> *"I am so sorry that I have to share this information with you however, this evening your husband Robert was involved in an auto accident and as a result of his injuries he did not survive the accident."*

Some responders are uncomfortable with performing a notification and will tend to draw out the process, which can cause additional emotional harm and trauma to the recipient. No matter how you present the notification, as the presenter you cannot change the outcome of events. Therefore, it is imperative that you notify the person (s) providing them with the basic information of events as soon as possible to help the family to begin the grieving process. The family may want to know more details about the event, and it is at that point that you will want to provide them with a person of contact who will be more equipped and qualified to answer their questions. As a first responder, you may be privy to graphic details of the event; however, it may not be your place to provide that information. If the recipient asks for more details, you can respond by saying,

> *"This is all the information I can give you at this time, however I can give you the name of a person to contact who will be able provide you with more details regarding the event."*

The survivor may want to view the body(s)

Survivors may request an opportunity to view the body of their loved one for a final time before removal. Survivors should be informed of the condition of the deceased before viewing, especially if the deceased died by suicide or a traffic accident. The chaplain should caution survivors and let them know that viewing the deceased in his or her current condition will leave a lasting image that will be etched into their memory. The question the chaplain should ask the survivor is if they prefer to remember the deceased as they were or as they are in their current condition. Ultimately, the choice will be theirs to make.

The following is a list of protocols that should be followed during the notification process.

1. The responders should clearly identify themselves, what agency they represent and present their credentials.
2. The responders should have the correct identity of the survivors before performing a notification.
3. If possible do not perform the notification on the doorstep.
4. Ask the survivor (s) to be seated.
5. Request that underage children leave the room.
6. Young children should be notified separately if possible, and if requested by the family.
7. Give the death notification directly and in plain language.
8. Call the deceased by name–rather than "the body."
9. Answer the survivor's questions directly
10. If you do not know the answer to a question, say so.

After the notification is complete, you may be asked to provide pastoral aftercare. Many new chaplains make the mistake of imposing their personal religious belief by making such statements as,

- "It was God's will"
- "She led a full life"
- "I understand what you are going through"

While those statements may have been presented with good intentions, during a tragedy, it may sound to some as condescending and insensitive, minimizing the person's moment of grief. The reality is that every person approach death and dying in different ways and regardless of our own experiences, we may not be able to identify with that person and truly know what they are emotionally experiencing. If the notification is suicide related do not be afraid to use the word "suicide." It is important when performing a death notification that it is done in an unbiased non-judgmental manner.

DEATH NOTIFICATION RECOMMENDATIONS IN THE WORKPLACE

- Ask to speak to the manager or supervisor
- Ask if the person to be notified is available
- Ask the manager or supervisor to arrange for a private room
- Allow the survivor time to react to the news and respond with your support
- Let the survivor determine what he or she wishes to tell the manager or supervisor regarding the death

DEATH NOTIFICATION RECOMMENDATIONS IN A HOSPITAL SETTING

The principles of death notification described above apply in the hospital setting. Here are several additional points: Find a quiet room in which the notification can be made and be sure the survivor(s) are seated.

(Do not make the notification in a crowded hall or waiting room.)

- ✓ If possible, arrange for a doctor to be present or available shortly after to answer medical questions or concerns
- ✓ Provide assistance and guidance
- ✓ Ask survivor(s) if they wish to spend time with the body of their loved one

- ✓ Refer the media to the investigating officer or victim service advocate
- ✓ Do not leave survivors alone
- ✓ Make certain someone always accompanies them
- ✓ Contact the survivor(s) the next day
- ✓ Optional: Make certain that the survivor(s) has your name and telephone number

DEBRIEFING AFTER A DEATH NOTIFICATION

The Death Notification team members should meet as soon as possible afterward for debriefing.

If possible, compete a peer review of the notification process, review what went wrong, what went right, and how can it be done better in the future. Share personal feelings and emotions. Death notifications are, without a doubt, stressful and often depressing. The notification experience may have triggered emotions within the first responder.

Follow-up:

Officer Suicide

When it comes to officer-involved suicides, contact those closest to the officer such as beat partners, department personnel, and family members.

Encourage co-workers to contact the deceased's family

It is extremely important for the survivors to try to put the "pieces" together to help better understand the events that lead to the suicide.

Expect Anger

- Do not be afraid to talk about the individual
- Reflect upon the way they lived, as well as the way they died.

HOW SURVIVORS RESPOND TO DEATH NOTIFICATION (PHYSICAL SHOCK)

Persons learning of the death may experience the following symptoms

- Tremors
- Sudden decrease in blood pressure
- Shock is a medical emergency–help should be Summoned
- In many cases the survivor may show no emotion
- Intensity of the event (I.e., violent death vs. heart attack)

Information

Attain as much information about the survivor's medical and emotional history before performing a notification. If a survivor suffers from emotional or physical ailments, that is a consideration that must be factored into the notification process.

Other general reactions to death notification

Even if there is no physical or emotional response, the death of a loved one creates a crisis for the surviving family member(s). Allow family members to express their feelings. Most likely, they will need help in determining what steps they need to take next. This may include additional notifications to other family members and funeral arrangements. *National Sheriffs association – Chaplains Reference Guide*

REPORTING AGENCY

____
____
____

Death Notification Form

NAME OF THE PERSON WHO HAS DIED	CAUSE OF DEATH
NAME OF AGENCY OR PERSON WHO REPORTED THE DEATH	TIME OF DEATH
NAME (S) OF THE PERSON NOTIFIED	RELATIONSHIP TO THE PERSON (S)

CIRCUMSTANCES SURROUNDING THE DEATH		
NOTIFIED BY	NOTIFICATION DATE	NOTIFICATION TIME
EMOTIONAL CONCERNS		
RESOURCES GIVEN AND RECOMMENDATIONS MADE		
NOTES:		

Student Notes

Part 4

The Process of Biblical Counseling

Biblical Counseling 101

The most significant portion of this book consists of Biblical Counseling, for a good reason. Proper Biblical counseling techniques is more than quoting scriptures and sharing platitudes. Instead, it is the art of reaching people at a personal and spiritual level. The two critical components to successful chaplaincy are (1) mastering the art of communication and (2) mastering the art of biblical counseling. In order to implement the techniques discussed in this book, you must first learn how to communicate your thoughts and actions. Whether performing a death notification, speaking with public officials, or developing personal relationships, communication plays a vital role. Excellent communication skills are the delivery system by which we can minister the Gospel of Christ and minister to people who are in crises or in need of simple guidance. The process of Biblical counseling is how we connect humanity to spirituality, and the Word of God is the conduit. This counseling model is designed to be used both in a pastoral church setting and in the field during community chaplaincy.

Lesson 8

Biblical Counseling 101

There are times in life when everyone faces personal loss, change, failures, abandonment, pain, suffering, and hopelessness. Feelings of loss, isolation, and separateness from others, from God, often occur in these difficult times. This often leads people to further destructive behaviors or to lose faith in God. At times when self-reliance has fallen short, people often reach out to others in the hope of finding help and guidance to lead them out of the darkness. Some of our brethren are going through one of life's many ordeals and are looking for someone to bring God's love, healing, hope, support, and direction. What are we called to do as Christians?

As Christians, we are first called to love one another, doing so by bearing one another burdens. God uses us to not only comfort those in need but also to use the Scripture to confront, rebuke, exhort, teach, and counsel others as discussed in Paul's Second Letter to Timothy, Chapter 3 verse 16. The word counsel (Greek prosthesis) means "a lying out beforehand" like a blueprint or a plan. This blueprint is not ours but from God. God has a plan for every soul He created, even during difficult times. Counselors must anchor themselves in the Word of God, as they provide love and guidance to those who are suffering, helping them to overcome their personal hardships. This course aims to equip the minister with Biblical guidance and teachings, which is foundational in Christian counseling. It will show that Biblical Counseling is a God-centered approach to helping suffering people come to an understanding that all answers and correction to the human condition is found in the Holy Bible. Often, emotional, and spiritual problems are the reflections of our sin nature and require acceptance and accountability on the part of the individual.

Often, we think of counseling in terms of clinical psychology, relying upon extra-biblical theories and treatments to achieve a cure to emotional trauma. Sigmund Freud, the father of modern psychology (meaning the study of the soul), defined the process of secular counseling as a medical discipline, treating the ailments of human emotions void of any spiritual reference. Biblical counseling, while spiritually based may mirror some aspects of clinical psychology since the research and the observance of the human condition reveals the attributes of human nature. Some portions of psychology may be integrated into spiritual care. However, there must be a dividing line between the counselor and the clinician, and the treatment aspect of counseling is best left to the licensed practitioner. The counselor is likened to a Life Coach, providing spiritual guidance, and counseling rather than administering a treatment-based program. For example, the Counselor may be involved in the lives of his or her parishioners throughout a lifetime, ministering to all aspects of their lives, including marriage relationships, domestic abuse, addressing stages of adolescence and more as opposed to the clinician who diagnoses symptoms and seeks a cure. In contrast, the counselor ministers to the individual, helps them to re-establish their relationship with God, and brings them to a place of contentment and peace in their life.

DO I NEED CLINICAL PASTORAL EDUCATION UNITS? (CPE)

Clinical Pastoral Education was introduced during mid-1920s by Rev. Anton T. Boisen, a former mental patient who was appointed as the institutional chaplain at the Worcester State Hospital, (Worcester, MA). Boisen, a former resident was first admitted as a patient as a result of having a mental breakdown. During his time spent as a chaplain Boisen incorporated a clinical approach to mental health that became the inspiration for many health professionals who endorsed the CPE program, which is widely received today as a standard in the healthcare industry for professional clergy.

Originally developed for the healthcare industry more and more employers are requiring that their chaplains have a minimum of one to four units of Clinical Pastoral Education Training before being considered for employment. In general, these requirements do not apply to chaplains who are not being monetarily compensated and who are serving as volunteers, except for the military reserves. For some students' classes can take an emotional toll. Students participate in 100 hours of didactic lectures accompanied by interactive Peer Reviews where they dissect and analyze each other's personal encounters with patients. Students also are required to provide a personal biography of their life, a self-portrait if you will, of their emotional upbringing and past experiences which is evaluated during peer review to determine if past experiences *(Transference vs counter transference)* play a role during a patient encounter. Participants must contribute a minimum of 300 intern hours at a local hospital or qualified healthcare facility putting into practice their CPE training.

CPE PROS AND CONS

CPE training is not a theologically based program per se but rather a component of psychology, which provides applications that, can be integrated into the pastoral realm of counseling. Teachings by qualified instructors may vary according to their religious persuasion which can provide a positive or negative learning experience leaving potential students with the tasked of determining if the teaching model is right for them. In one instance, it was reported that a CPE instructor who was teaching a semester to a group of Christian ministers would not allow his students to discuss or incorporate any Christian principles into their live practicums. The instructor, an ordained minister and chaplain struggled with his own faith, which was the basis for his prohibition, and which created difficulties among the class participants. Another report revealed that one instructor who had strong New Age convictions integrated those beliefs into his class sessions, which resulted in many of the class participants embracing these concepts. Many instructors in the world of CPE believe that clergy who do not possess CPE units are not qualified to serve as a chaplain or in some cases a pastor, which is an uneducated point of view and is misleading. To understand Clinical Pastoral Education training, the student must grasp the life and world of the chaplain. Chaplaincy is broken down into several subcategories and requires a host of different teachings, understanding and skill levels in order for the chaplain to perform his or her duty. The old saying that states, "There is a time and a place for all things" holds true when it comes to CPE, Christian counseling, and any form of clinical response. Often, during a crisis, circumstances may dictate the need of chaplaincy as a ministry of presence rather than an onsite counseling session.

Clinical Pastoral Education can be best described as an educational component of chaplaincy, a tool. However, is not the basis by which chaplaincy is established, succeeds, or fails. I am not opposed to Clinical Pastoral Education training and firmly believe that it provides a good opportunity to increase one's clinical knowledge however, it is imperative that the "Pastoral" component in Clinical Pastoral Education is observed and followed otherwise the student may well be straying into a realm of clinical psychology where he or she may be unduly qualified. I do believe that CPE training can be an asset and a valuable tool for the chaplain. However, it must be understood in proper context.

MOVING FORWARD – THE FIVE-STEP PROCESS OF BIBLICAL COUNSELING

In this lesson, we will learn about the five steps of Biblical counseling and the emotional framework and expectation of the counselee. There are **two basic goals** in Biblical based counseling. First helping the individual address their concerns from a Biblical perspective and second, guiding the person through the stages of Biblical development using the Five Step process of Biblical Counseling. The following topics offer a pathway to successful counseling practice.

STEPS 1-ESTABLISHING RELATIONSHIP WITH THE INDIVIDUAL EMPLOYING THE FOLLOWING METHODS

- Empathy
- Respect
- Trust

STEP 2- COLLECTING INFORMATION

1. Gathering information about the counselee by using communication, auditory, and observations skills
2. Collecting and documentation
3. Using data gathering tools such as the Personal Discovery Assignment Form (PDA) and the Extensive Data Gathering Question Form (EDGQ)

STEP 3- UNDERSTANDING THE PROBLEMS

1. Analyze and discover problem patterns
2. Use Discover Problem Pattern (PDD) Form
3. Provide counselees with a conceptual understanding of ANGER and GUILT

STEP 4-BIBLICAL PROCESS OF CHANGE (FIVE R'S)

1. **Responsibility** for personal thoughts, desires attitudes, words, and actions.
2. **Repentance** for sinful thoughts and actions

3. **Reconciliation** with God and those involved, by confession of sins, asking for forgiveness from those we have harmed, and forgiving others who have harmed us.
4. **Renewal** of the mind by developing an awareness of thoughts and actions that promote sinful behavior, putting off those desires that hinder biblical change and replacing them with ones that promote biblical transformation.
5. **Replacement** of old habits with good new habits.

STEP 5- MAINTAINING CHANGE (ACRONYM "ACCEPT")

A – Acknowledge personal responsibility for thoughts and actions
C – Choose to live by biblical principles in all circumstances.
C – Commit to a plan to eliminate whatever hinders biblical change.
E – Execute the plan with energy toward the goals set.
P – Persevere in obedience to Biblical principles.
T – Trust God for the strength and resources for change

The goals of biblical counseling are two folds:

1. Help the counselee understand their issues from Biblical perspective.
2. Induce the Biblical process of change in counselee.

TYPES OF COUNSELING INDIVIDUAL

When providing counsel to those in need, the counselor is likely to come upon two types of personalities that can dramatically affect the outcome of a counseling session if not recognized and addressed accordingly.

1. The talker individual
2. The reluctant individual

The "talkers"-some individuals are quick to offer information and may appear to be very agreeable though the information provided may be unrelated or irrelevant to the conversation at hand. Such individuals often avoid addressing problems as a result of their fear of having to confront painful and deep-seated issues. The counselee may already be committed to the idea that he or she is correct regarding the situation and that the other person is the one with the problem. We find this type of deflecting common among couples during counseling, leaving the counselor with the task of directing the conversation to neutral grounds.

The "reluctant" tend to hold back their feelings and emotions, leaving the Counselor to pry information out of the counselee, thus making it difficult for counselor s to help them address their issues. Most individuals are at this opposite extreme, so we will focus our attention and skills on this type of counselee. To be effective at gathering information from this type of counselee, the counselor must recognize that there are barriers to overcome, understanding the person we are trying to help before delving into specific issues. Some people are reluctant to share personal information because they feel embarrassed about their situation.

Some people may be a concerned that the counselor will be biased due to their religious perspective and beliefs and fear being alienated and disrespected. In the church, there may be more liberties when it comes to spiritual discipline and expectations since it is likely that a person who is seeking counseling in a church setting may be somewhat grounded in the disciplines of the faith. However, when counseling a non-believer, spiritual principles may be applied while church doctrines may be irrelevant. The counselor tasked with helping the individual open the door to their inner world of fears, emotions and pain, where they will often discover the roots of their social and emotional problems.

COMMON REASONS FOR SEEKING COUNSELING

There are moments in people's lives when they come to the realization that they are lost, unable to resolve the personal crisis on their own and need outside help. Some reach out for help from the pastoral community, and it is at these moments of vulnerability that the counselor must be sensitive to their emotional and spiritual needs. The following are some of the common problems facing people in today's society.

- Family problems regarding children
- Marital problems
- Conflict resolution
- Drugs or alcohol abuse
- Sexual difficulty
- Difficulty at work/school/ career
- Moral or ethical dilemma
- Faith based issues
- Health issues
- Financial difficulties

Some people may approach us with a concern that requires immediate attention or a prompt referral to a healthcare professional, i.e., psychiatrist, psychologist, or medical doctor. Some things are beyond the scope of this introductory course in Biblical counseling.

The following are examples of situations that may require a professional referral.

- Grief and Bereavement *(Additional training may be needed for this specific type of counseling)*
- Severe clinical depression *(Immediate referral to a healthcare professional may be necessary)*

- Suicidal intentions *(When the threat of suicide is verbalized, emergency intervention from a healthcare professional or 911 interventions are required)*
- Mental breakdowns require immediate attention.

A conventional theory among Christian believers is that all psychological issues are quickly resolved through biblical intervention and that a lack of progress reflects a lack of faith in a person's life. Faulty thinking is often the result of a lack of counseling experience. Thus, hiding behind religious legalism and mandates seemly provides a quick answer to a deep-rooted problem. Clearly, God is the restorer of the human soul and through supernatural miracles can bring about healing in all situations. However, we cannot discount that God may use an alternate approach to emotional healing by utilizing clinical and medical professionals during seasons of life. Therefore, bizarre, and unusual behaviors must be further evaluated by the counselor to determine if there is a concern that requires immediate medical attention. Counselors should not assign a psychological diagnosis to the counselee (e.g., psychotic or schizophrenic) unless they are trained and licensed clinicians.

Student Notes

Lesson 9

The Building Blocks of Counseling

ESTABLISHING RELATIONSHIP - In the last lesson, our discussion covered the topic regarding the most common types of counselees, particularly those who are reluctant and avoid addressing personal issues. We discovered at the root of their concerns was an embarrassment, fear of being misunderstood or judged, being shunned, or disrespected, and the loss of reputation. This lesson covers the first step in the Five-Step Process of Biblical Counseling, which begins with establishing relationships between the counselor and the counselee. The development and maintenance of a trusting and facilitative relationship or professional friendship between the counselor and counselee are paramount if we are going to make a difference. The Counselor must develop an atmosphere of trust and compassion, avoid lecturing, talking about others or ourselves but instead focus on the counselees and their needs. The gage of our influence in the lives of others to whom we provide counsel is often based on their perception of us as people of faith. Let us look at the three building blocks needed to build a strong relationship with the counselee.

- Empathy
- Respect
- Trust

EMPATHY

The concept of empathy is best described as understanding the individual and his or her concern from their personal perspective. It is not to suggest that the counselor should agree or condone a person's bad behavior if that were the reason for seeking biblical counseling. Counselors must be careful to empathize with the person rather than sympathize. While sympathy is not necessarily wrong, it lays the groundwork for the counselor to become emotionally involved in the matter, thus creating a bias towards the situation. For example, if the counselor is providing marriage counseling to a couple, his own opinion and bias regarding the topic of adultery may cause him sympathizes with the perceived victim and become prejudice towards the perpetrator rather than addressing the original reason for the session, which was the restoration of the marriage. Another area of concern is counseling a person who is dealing with the issue of grief or responding to a major crisis where there is a great deal of trauma and emotion, thus running the risk of becoming emotionally involved with the event, leading to secondary trauma on the part of the counselor.

Does Jesus really sympathize with us in our time of need?

In the previous paragraph, we discussed the topic of empathy vs. sympathy. Yet, there are moments in life when offering sympathy to a person in crisis is appropriate such as in the sudden loss of a family member or close friend. In this case, personal involvement is unavoidable.

The Bible recounts the story of Jesus as having compassion toward those who are in need.

> Hebrews 4:15, the Bible states, *"For we do not have a High Priest who cannot sympathize with our weakness, but was in all points tempted as we are, yet without sin. "*

There are times when sharing the person's emotional pain demonstrates care and commitment toward others and builds a bond between the counselor and counselee. It is the personalization of events that will determine whether a counselor should refer the session to another provider who is less involved. Another example is a law enforcement chaplain who once commented saying that throughout a given month he would perform five to six death notifications to complete strangers. In this instance, the chaplain said he could only empathize with the grieving families to avoid the transference of grief and of becoming emotionally incapacitated.

Empathy - Do not react too quickly

During counseling, it is crucial to resist the impulse to quickly interpret their story and offer reasons for why they are suffering and experiencing pain. Avoid Christian clichés such as "It's all part of God's will" or "God lets things happen for a reason" which can sound like an insult. It is vital to help the counselee understand that bad things happened for a reason as we are subjected to unfortunate and unavoidable events in our lives while other events and outcomes are the result of cause and effect and are preventable.

How are we to show empathy to others?

Empathizing with someone who is going through a crisis requires us to express compassion towards the person in his or her situation. It is the most loving act we could do for someone and is a trait that we, as counselors, should cultivate. The Bible gives us the following guidance in developing our compassion toward others:

- Think about how we would feel if we were in the counselee's position
- Treat the counselee as a family member
- Acknowledge our own capacity for sin
- Demonstrate genuine love and compassion toward the counselee

Acknowledge our own capacity for sin

Apostle Paul instructs in his letter to the Galatians by stating:

✞ *"Brethren, even if a man is caught in any trespass, you who are spiritual, restore such a one in a spirit of gentleness; considering yourself, lest you too be tempted. Galatians" 6:1*

When addressing the issues of sinful behavior in the life of the individual, it is essential to remember that we also are not immune to the trap of immoral behavior. A healthy understanding will help us to avoid becoming overly self-righteous or condescending toward those whom we care for, particularly those who are dealing with sensitive issues.

Compassion is a choice

Compassion is not so much an emotion as it is a choice, choosing to minister to those with whom we may have disagreements, doing so despite our own personal feelings.

> ***Jesus instructed his followers:*** *"Love your enemies, do good to those who hate you, bless those who curse you, and pray for those who spitefully use you". (Luke 6:27-28)*

Jesus does instruct us to show compassion based on our personal feelings.

The Bible provides an outline for conduct and success

- ✞ Letting the counselees know that we care for them (Philemon 1:8)
- ✞ Praying for the counselee and their situation (Colossians 4:12-13)
- ✞ Rejoicing in their victories and grieving with them during their distress (Romans 12:15)
- ✞ Dealing with them gently and tenderly (Matthew 12:20)
- ✞ Being tactful with them (Proverbs 15:33)
- ✞ Speaking graciously to them (Colossians 4:6)
- ✞ Defending them against those who mistreat and accuse them (Matt. 12:1-7)
- ✞ Forgiving them for any wrong they have done to us (Matthew 18:21-22)
- ✞ Continuing to love and accept them even when they have rejected our counsel (Mark 10:21)

RESPECT

Embarrassment, fear, being ridiculed and a loss of reputation are often emotional barriers that prevent people from seeking out biblical counseling. To overcome such boundaries, there must be a mutual understanding and respect between the counselor and the counselee. This holds true when providing counsel to someone who is incarcerated, who has expressed a desire for change and who is seeking out spiritual counsel. A criminal past does not necessarily deny the possibility of change, therefore; the counselor who may think that change is not possible must reconsider his thinking and opinions in order not to create an atmosphere of disrespect.

The Bible suggest several ways in which to show respect to people that will help us in developing meaningful and fruitful relationships.

- Using proper verbal communication
- Expressing appropriate non-verbal communication
- Taking counselee's problems seriously

We can show respect to our counselee by the way we communicate. The Apostol Paul counsels the church, *"A servant of the Lord must not quarrel but be gentle to all, able to teach, patient, in humility correcting those who are in opposition, if God perhaps will grant them repentance, so that they may know the truth."* (2 Timothy 2:24-25) Rude, harsh, or condemning speech is never condoned in Scripture, even when speaking the truth.

Use appropriate non-verbal communication

Counselor s should be aware that disrespect could be manifested in body language such as in the folding of arms or appearing distance or indifferent. Poor posture, facial, and expressions may convey an entirely different message to the counselee and overshadow that which has verbalized positively.

The following is a list of communication guidelines

1. Sit at the same eye level as the counselee as not to look down at them.
2. Facing the counselee directly conveys that we are giving them our full attention.
3. Relaxing our arms, hands, and shoulders, avoid crossing arms.
4. Leaning slightly forward – communicates interest in what counselee has to say.
5. Speak at a volume that reflects tenderness and compassion.
6. Eye contact–show interest by looking at the counselee, never stare.
7. Avoid facial grimaces or expressions that communicate disapproval, anger, or condescending.

TAKE THE COUNSELEE'S PROBLEMS SERIOUSLY

It is often a challenge to work with people who are experiencing significant emotional behavior, mainly if the event seems trivial. The counselor should cautiously avoid minimizing the problem or emotional trauma experienced by the counselee regardless of their bias. The person experiencing a loss, job change, or any other emotional experience, the trauma is real and overwhelming. Example: in the United States a family pet, is often viewed, as an actual member of the family and any illness or loss can be a devastating moment in the lives of those coping with the loss. Immigrants from third world countries often view pets such as cats and dogs as personal property rather than a member of the family; thus, any emotional attachment to the pet is limited.

Trust - In developing a therapeutic and rehabilitative relationship, trust is a crucial requirement. Trust demands respect and honesty when entering a counseling relationship. Trust requires that the counselor maintain strict confidentiality in all matters of conversation and is absolutely necessary for the counselee to feel comfortable about revealing their problems and darkest concerns. The following acronym (HLC) can serve as an important reminder.

- Honesty
- Loyalty
- Confidentiality

Honesty – In therapeutic relationships, honesty is a crucial component, and without it, personal rehabilitation is likely to be unsuccessful. As counselor s, we may not always have solutions to the problem or even the experience to address the issue that has been presented by the counselee. In such circumstances, it is appropriate to address the counselee by stating, "That is a question that requires additional research, so please allow me an opportunity to do some homework on the matter." This demonstrates that the relationship between the counselor and the counselee is based on a foundation of honesty and truth instilling a sense of confidence and reliability towards the counselor while offering greater opportunities and solutions. Openness towards the counselee in personal matters of concern is also an essential part of the rehabilitation process. The counselor must avoid the appearance of condoning inappropriate behavior or treading lightly in areas of sensitivity.

> *Be honest in your estimate of yourself... Good people are guided by their honesty. Proverb 11:3*

Confidentiality - In recent years, there has been an increasing number of lawsuits filed against clergy for the invasion of privacy arising out of the disclosure of confidential information acquired during counseling sessions with parishioners. The result of these suits has brought about more scrutiny when it comes to confidentiality and the release of personal information.

Student Notes

Lesson 10

Gathering Information part I

In Step 1 - of the Biblical counseling process, the counselors have broken through the initial barrier, established a relationship with the counselee, and gained access to their inner world. The successful counselor developed this relationship through building on a foundation empathy, respect, and trust.

In Step 2 - The counselor is tasked with the systematic gathering of information using the Personal Assessment Form resource material if available. A rush to judgment should be avoided before having all the available information. Otherwise, the counselor runs the risk miss diagnosing the issue, making matters worse and to an already stressful situation. During this phase of the counseling process, the counselor should encourage the counselee to share as much information as possible while listening and take notes. For successful biblical counseling to occur, the counselor must develop skillful and organized methods of gaining information.

There are three skills that every effective counselor must learn:

- Listening to and observing the counselee
- Asking appropriate questions
- Not jumping to conclusions

The most important skill to be utilized by the counselor is exercising the ability to be a good listener, who is at the heart of human communication. Listening is an essential component when attempting to collect relevant information. The Bible reminds us to "be swift to hear, slow to speak..." (James 1:19) and encourages us that "the mind of the prudent acquires knowledge and ears of the wise seeks knowledge." (Proverbs 18:15). Listen for facts before acting on assumptions.

> *"He who answers a matter before he hears it, It is folly and shame to him" (Proverbs 18:13)*

Doctrinal interference: Religious doctrine can be a sticking point for many care providers and is often the reason for the breakdown in communication between the counselor and the counselee. This is symptomatic of highly legalistic churches where the interpretation of doctrine prevails over biblical teachings. For example, a counselee who is dealing with a reoccurring drug addiction problem where there are significant identifiable triggers such as the person's social setting and family structure. During a counseling session, the counselor may offer counsel based on doctrinal precepts rather than addressing the counselee's emotional baggage, thus limiting the opportunity for real recovery.

🕮 ***Case study - 1:*** John, a recovering drug addict, attended a local church where he sought out Christian counseling for his addiction, reaching out to the senior counselor for emotional and spiritual help. The counselor grounded in denominational and legalistic doctrine lacked experience in biblical counseling, relied upon his doctrinal beliefs and suggested that John's struggle with drug addiction was simply due to his lack of faith in God and not trusting God to bring about true healing. As a result, the counselor dismissed John's social and emotional triggers as a non-factor in the recovery process and based his conclusions

> instead on his interpretation of religious doctrine. This led John to believe that due to his perceived lack of faith and his inability to address his addiction or find an adequate solution for recovery, John left the church and returned to his life of drug use.

While faith plays a vital role in the life of the believer, a lack of counseling experience should never be a reason for minimizing the counselee's problems, lifestyle choices, and compulsive behavior. If the counselor lacks counseling experience or is not comfortable with addressing the situation, an option for a referral should be in place.

Examples of clergy who are required minister in a non-religious setting (Leaving their doctrinal beliefs at the front door) are hospital chaplains, many who encounter patients from different religious and nonreligious backgrounds. In an interdenominational environment, the chaplain must be prepared to address the patients' needs regardless of faith or belief. It is incumbent upon the chaplain to utilize his Christian counseling skills void of any mention of religious doctrine. For many counselors, this is a difficult concept to follow. The counselor must learn to incorporate biblical principles into a non-religious setting without compromising his faith. Fortunately, the Bible addresses most if not all, of life's issues that plague the human emotion. It has been reported that many non-religious people who underwent counseling (Faith was not part of the discussion) were often unaware that the final resolution to their problem was grounded on biblical principles. Therefore, the integration of the biblical tenets during the counseling of a non-religious person can be achieved while effectively minister the healing Gospel of Jesus Christ.

Understanding the counselee

Interaction between the counselor and counselee can sometimes be vague and uneventful due to the flow of conversation. During a counseling session, the counselor needs to listen to what the counselee is saying, such as the person's use of language and terms, and then discover the meaning between the lines. Often what a person is actually saying is not what is being expressed. For example, during a recent couples counseling session, the wife stated that she was angry and frustrated towards her husband and complained that he never took out the trash. After some additional probing, the wife was asked if this had been a problem in the past, and she responded by stating that there had been no prior conflicts regarding the matter. Further discussion revealed that the actual reason for her anger towards her husband had to do with her husband's lack of appreciation for her efforts and availability around the home.

When asking questions, there different levels of response that can reveal what is truly in the heart and mind of the counselee as demonstrated below and the trigger that led to that response.

1. ***"I am angry"***

   This level of response reveals a particular trigger for the feeling/behavior.

2. ***"I am angry with myself because I hit my wife."***

   The deepest level of response illuminates the underlying behavior pattern.

3. ***"I am angry with myself because I can't seem to control my temper when my wife tries to control me!"***

Navigating superficial levels of response

The individual may be reluctant to reveal their true feelings and may respond to questions posed by the counselor by providing a partial response. In general, a partial answer is the end result of the counselor asking a close-ended question. It is incumbent upon the counselor to probe deeper, asking the counselee relevant and open-ended questions. Once the counselor has determined an underlying cause to the issue in question, he must explore what options have been taken by the counselee to address the problem.

The art of active listening

- Structure the sessions to elicit information from the counselee –Counselors must seek to clarify answers that are vague or superficial, listen for, and elicit specific information.
- Control the flow of the talk – The counselor must exercise sensitivity when interviewing the counselee. Some people may be addressing a sensitive issue for the first time, which can be a very traumatic moment in a person's life.

Listen beyond attitudes and feelings – This is very important when gathering information. Counselors should use reflective remarks and response techniques to acquire more information that is specific.

Reflective Remarks and Responses Techniques

This technique aid, the counselor, and challenge the counselee to avoid responding using vague language to express their emotions. As a counselor, you will want to navigate the flow of conversation to achieve an appropriate response. The following is a short example of how to redirect negative comments by the counselee.

Counselee: "I can't"

Counselor: Do you mean can't or you won't? According to Scripture, it says you can

Counselee: "I did everything I could."

Counselor: Everything, what about … (Offer an alternative)

Counselee: "I've tried what you suggested but it didn't work."

Counselor: Did you really try, if so, how many times? How persistent were you in your efforts?

Counselee: "I did my best."

Counselor: Are you sure, can you tell me precisely what you did?

Counselee: "I could never do that."

Counselor: Never is a long time, perhaps you can learn.

Counselee: "If I had the time, I'd do it."

Counselor: We all have 24 hours each day to do what we need to do. It all depends on how you organize your day. Now let us work on drawing up a schedule that honors GOD.

Counselee: "Don't blame me"

Counselor: Are you saying you are not responsible for your actions?

Counselee: "Don't ask me!"

Counselor: But I am asking you, who else would know? I am sure that you know the answer.

Counselee: "I guess so"

Counselor: Are you really guessing or is it that what you believe?

Counselee: "You know how it is!"

Counselor: Not really, can you explain it more fully so I can understand?

Counselee: "I've prayed about it!"
Counselor: "Great, what exactly did you pray for and what does the Bible say about the problem?

Counselee: "I'm at the end of my rope"
Counselor: Perhaps you are beginning to uncoil your problems for the first time.

Counselee: "I have needs too!"
Counselor: You need or want or perhaps it is a habitual problem.

Counselee: "I'm just one of those people"
Counselor: Yes, I am sure you are but Christ wants you to become a different person.

Counselee: "That's just the way I am, I can't help it"
Counselor: Are you saying that God does not have the power to change you?

Counselee: "That's impossible!"
Counselor: Perhaps you mean difficult.
Counselee: "You can't teach an old dog new trick."
Counselor: Perhaps that is true, but you are not a dog. You were created in the image and likeness of GOD! He knows you and commands you to change.

Counselee: "It will never work."
Counselor: You should never say never, rather it is better to try and fail than to not to try at all.

Counselee: "Everything or everyone is against me."
Counselor: God's word tells us, "IF GOD be for us, who can be against us?" (Romans 8:31)

LISTENING TO ALL THE FACTS (HALO DATA)

The information we seek does not only come from words that we hear, but also from information, that is communicated non-verbally, also known as (HALO DATA) paralinguistic communication.

Human Behavior

✞ Genesis 3:8 says, "*The man and his wife hid themselves from the presence of the LORD GOD among the trees of the garden.*"

In this verse, Adam and Eve expressed emotions for their wrongdoing and shame. They did not have to say one word, yet they were plagued with guilt, and fear, from disobeying God's command regarding eating from the Tree of Knowledge of Good and Evil. During biblical counseling, we can learn much by observing body language and facial expressions. Facial expressions can reveal discomfort, anger, sorrow, or other debilitating emotions. Sometimes people will fidget or involuntarily cross their arms in front of their chest or avoid eyes contact. These are possible indicators can reveal pertinent information about the person and maybe useful during the counseling session.

PARA-LINGUISTIC COMMUNICATION

This level of Para-Linguistic Communication (Halo Data) has to do with primarily with how a person speaks and how they express their emotions. The tone of voice, sudden hesitation, and choice of words can reflect their current emotional state and can uncover valuable information. The tone of voice can communicate hope and despair. It can reveal a person's level of anxiety or if the individual is emotionally in a good place. Other concerns include anger, forgiveness, love or hate, interest, or indifference. Halo Data can also provide useful information that can help the counselor navigate the conversation.

For example (Questions)

- "When I asked you that question you seemed uncomfortable. Could you help me understand what bothered you about the question?"
- "You seem upset today was it something I had said, or have I done something to upset you?
- "You seem a little preoccupied what are you thinking about?"

ASKING APPROPRIATE QUESTIONS

The counselor should avoid asking invasive questions that are not relevant to the conversation, and when addressing sensitive issues, it should be done with absolute respect and sensitivity towards the counselee. The following information will provide the counselor with some useful guidelines.

Thoughtful Line of Questioning

✝ The Bible teaches, *"Let your speech always be with grace, seasoned, as it were, with salt" (Colossians 4:6).*

Whether conducting marriage counseling or counseling an individual, the counselor's line of questioning should be thoughtful and well thought out before beginning a session. The counselor must take the time to explain to the counselee what type of questions will be asked and why and explain how the questions are relevant to the conversation. When introducing a subject for discussion, the counselor can use the advance-and-retreat method of communication. If the counselee becomes apprehensive or is uncomfortable with the line of questioning, the counselor may temporarily discontinue the line of questioning and revisit the topic at a later time.

Relevant questions

The counselor's line of questioning should always be relevant to the topic of discussion and subsequent questions arising from the conversation should flow from previous answers given by the counselee. The counselor should avoid questions that may be perceived by the counselee as a question asked out of curiosity.

Some suggestions and conversational tips

Avoid questions that start with "WHY." Usually, a question that begins with the word "WHY "tends to evoke speculation and put people on the defensive.

Make an effort to ask more of the "WHAT" type of questions because they tend to elicit facts. Generally, what type of questions produce more information than "why" questions.

Example:

- What is the problem?
- What happened? What do you mean?
- What have you done about it?
- What has helped?
- What made it worse?
- What do you think about…?

Helpful questions start with the word "HOW":

- How do you feel about …?
- How have you responded?
- How have you reacted?
- How have you tried to resolve it?
- How long have you had this problem?
- How often have you had it?
- How can I be of help?

Avoid accepting yes and no answers

Avoid interviewing the person by using a line of questioning that can be quickly answered with a quick YES or a NO. Questions should be "open-ended" so that the person cannot avoid the issue by hiding behind a yes or a no answer. On the other hand, open-ended questions encourage the individual to reveal more information and force a response by the person and addressing the issue. There are situations where yes or no types of answers are appropriate, for example, (1) When we want to get a commitment from a counselee (2) When we need to clarification and conformation. We need to be mindful of the kind of questions during counseling, and we need to choose them carefully so that they will provide the most information possible but be aware of the comfort level of the counselee.

The following are examples of open-ended questions

- **Instead of** - Do you want to get married?
- **Ask** - What are your thoughts about marriage?
- **Instead of** - Do you love your husband?
- **Ask** - How do you feel about your husband?
- **Instead of** - Are you satisfied with your job?
- **Ask** - What do you like or dislike about your job?

Counselors should not settle for generalizations or abstractions in the person's response. Answers should be exact, concrete, and specific as vague, superficial, or hypothetical answers rarely reveal much information. The counselor should always seek clarification when the person's responses are unclear. Halo-Data is a useful tool when seeking out clarification during the interview process.

Student Notes

Lesson 11

Gathering Information part 2

COLLECTING AND ORGANIZING INFORMATION RECEIVED

In the previous lesson, we learned what skills are needed to be a competent counselor and include being a good listener, close observation of the counselee, and asking appropriate questions. We learned about Halo-Data and Paralinguistic Communication, as well as how religious doctrine can play a role during the counseling session. This lesson will focus on the process of gathering relevant information. The type of information collected from the counselee can provide the counselor with a profile of the individual, their likes and dislikes, physical and mental health background, religious upbringing, among other relevant information. If the counselor is going to take notes during the counseling session, an explanation should be given, and the counselor should reaffirm that confidentiality is absolute.

THE KIND OF INFORMATION TO COLLECT

In this part of the lesson, we will explore the six (6) major components of a person life that could have tremendous impact and magnify their problems.

1. Physical Health
2. Emotion
3. Action
4. Concept
5. Personal History

PHYSICAL HEALTH

The success of our counsel will sometimes be dependent upon understanding a particular aspect of someone's health. We need to be aware of any outstanding physical issues the counselee may be dealing with as it can dramatically affect the ability of the counselee to address the problem. A person's physical condition can play a role and be a determining factor as to whether or not the person can take the next step in the recovery process. There are five (5) aspects of our physical lives that can influence our spiritual health:

Sleep patterns

It is estimated that the average individual needs approximately seven to eight hours of undisturbed sleep each night to function and perform well in their daily lives. Sleeping in excess may be an indicator that a person is suffering from a physical ailment or dealing with chronic depression, and prolonged sleep deprivation can lead to a mental breakdown. Sleep deprivation can lead to excessive fatigue, irritability, attention deficit, poor judgment, and erratic behavior. The high intake of caffeinated products in our society is often a contributing factor to a lack of sleep as well as sleep apnea, which should be addressed by a medical professional as soon as possible.

Diet and Exercise

Poor nutrition can affect behavior as well and is the root of physical illness, lack of energy, and emotional wellbeing. Before the industrial revolution, the rigors of life were more labor-intensive, and people were more physically active. Today, many jobs while stressful are not physically demanding to leave the individual with the responsibility of incorporating physical fitness into their busy lifestyle. Often, people fail to reach their fitness goals due to the distractions of life, where time is a precious commodity. Diet and exercise can play a vital role in our mental and physical wellbeing. A lack of exercise can contribute to heighten anxiety, physical illness, and mood disorders. Encouraging the counselee to start a regiment of diet and exercise can significantly help the counselee to relax and overcome their anxiety and stress.

Physical Illness

Sickness is often lifestyle (Such as alcoholism, drug use, and promiscuity) related, which can lead to depression, stomach ulcers, gastric disturbances, liver conditions, heart disease, and terminal illness.

Prescription and non-prescription medications

Various medications, both prescription and over-the-counter drugs, can cause emotional and physical side effects that are physically harmful. These drugs can contribute to ongoing problems, especially if the individual is not aware of the possibility of side effects. In some cases of mild depression, a physician can treat a patient by simply finding out what medication the person has been taking and making adjustments in dosage or eliminating use altogether. A counselor must learn to gather pertinent information and be prepared to make a referral to a medical professional when necessary.

Religious belief systems

During marriage counseling, the counselor may have one spouse who is of faith and the other spouse who may subscribe to a non-Christian belief system or profess no faith at all. Though it is not impossible to apply biblical principles when counseling a person who is not of faith, it is much easier to address the person's emotional needs if they have a Christian belief system. In the early stages of Christian counseling, a counselor must ascertain a person's level of faith and personal relationship with God, as it will guide the counselor, providing direction on how to address the situation.

RESOURCES

Resources such as handouts and referrals are essential when providing counseling services. Women dealing with domestic violence may need an immediate referral to women or family shelter, providing temporary relief from physical abuse to address the emotional issues of the situation. In the case of the sudden death of a family member, providing immediate referrals to mortuaries and cremation services can reduce the amount of emotional stress during a time of grief.

EMOTION

Emotions are a pivotal part of our human makeup and serve as a gage that informs us of how we feel now, about our lives or about a particularly stressful situation. For example, a parent knows that when a child acts out by expressing feelings through emotional outburst and tantrums, there is usually an underlining cause. Emotions can be constructive or unproductive in which case further research often reveals the underling stressor for that emotion. Constructive emotions are love, joy, feeling of wellbeing, and excitement. Unproductive emotions are uncontrolled rage, paranoia, feelings related to addictions, depression, and irritability.

A professional therapist may diagnose a patient and treat a symptom through medication; behavioral therapy yet fails to address the cause, which may be a lifestyle-related problem. For example, secular therapeutic professionals may view homosexuality as a positive lifestyle and ignore any spiritual conflicts the person may encounter. However, the Christian counselor who counsels a person who was raised, in a Christian home, now struggling with homosexual tendencies may view homosexuality as a conflict of lifestyle and a stressor thus recommending a change from a biblical perspective.

ACTION

The teachings of Scripture clearly link our choice of lifestyle and personal actions with other aspects of our lives, which can have a profound effect on our spiritual, emotional, and physical wellbeing. Disobedience to God's plan for healthy living can produce negative emotions such as guilt, grief, a sense of personal failure leading to a continuation of corrupt living.

- ✞ The Bible tells us, *"Behold, I set before you the way if life and the way of death." Jeremiah 21:8.*

CONCEPTS

The Bible provides us with wise counsel and teaches that life and daily living rooted in the Word of God provides us with a foundation for healthy living.

- *"For the Word of God is living and powerful, and sharper than a two-edged sword, piercing even the division of the soul and spirit, and of joint and marrow, and is a discerner of the thoughts and intentions of the heart.* Hebrews 4:12

Concepts include personal convictions, attitudes, expectations, desires, and values as well as,

1. What are people relying upon
2. What are they fearing?
3. Who are they listening too?
4. Whom, are they depending upon?
5. What motivates people's lives
6. What or who is in control of their lives.

As important as actions and emotions are, in a sense, they are secondary to our conceptual understanding of life because what we think, and desire (our thoughts and intentions) ultimately determines our feelings and actions.

- *"What comes out of man that defiles a man? For from within, out of the heart of men, proceed evil thoughts, adulteries, fornications, murders, thefts covetousness, wickedness, deceit, lewdness, an evil eye, blasphemy, pride, foolishness. All these things process from within and defile the man." Mark 7:20-23*

In Christian counseling, we must gain as much information about the counselee as possible to effectively minister to their personal emotional needs. The ultimate goal is to correct faulty thought patterns, misconceptions and help them achieve "the mind of Christ" (1 Corinthians 2:16)

PERSONAL HISTORY

Personal history is the gathering of information both past, present, and includes the following.

1. External circumstances affecting their lives
2. Influences or pressure they have experienced or are experiencing
3. Frustrations, hardships, failures, and temptations
4. Blessings, successes, comforts, and wealth

Other issues that need to be addressed include family origin, marital history, and other significant relationships, problems in school or family, and possible physical or sexual abuse. We need to be concerned about any shaping experiences from the past – especially those that the counselee believes are important.

- ✞ Modern psychology tends to place blame on the past due to the injustice committed against the patient such as child abuse, domestic violence, dysfunctional living, and poverty thus alleviating them from their duty to take personal responsibility for their actions. Former victims of child abuse and domestic violence are often themselves perpetrators of the same act of violence, citing past experience as a motivating factor. While having been a victim of abuse is an emotional and tragic event in a person's life, it does not validate or excuse bad behavior or personal responsibility.
- ✞ *"They will give an account to Him who is ready to judge the living and the dead." (1. Peter 4:5 NKJV)*

Biblical counselors must be cognizant that some information gathered may be irrelevant, inappropriate, clinical, sterile, and even hurtful and should be carefully sorted through. The counselor must be observant of people, and their living conditions, and environment since they often reveal the root of their stress and emotions. More information should be acquired about the person's marriage, family situations, personal relationships, church involvement, occupation, and personal finances.

INFORMATION COLLECTION TOOLS

Dr. Wayne A. Mack, Professor of Biblical Counseling at master's College, developed a set of resources to aid and guide, the Christian counselor during counseling, to collect personal information that will help the counselor gain a deeper understanding and provided a profile of the counselee. No two people are the same, and each may react differently in the same situation. People have different viewpoints when it comes to life, politics, sports, religion, likes, and dislikes, which can play a role in people's responses during the interview process.

For example, a couple seeking marriage counseling may come from two entirely different backgrounds and lifestyles. One may have been raised is a wealthy home, exposed to refinements and provided with educational opportunities while the other spouse may have come from a less progressive background of struggle and hardship where opportunities were limited. In this scenario, one spouse may feel conflict based on personal ideologies developed over the period and upbringing and introduce those ideas into the marriage while the other spouse may draw a different conclusion based on their perspective and view the other spouse as thoughtless and inconsiderate and seek a different outcome to the situation. The counselor's job is to help the couple seek a compromise, find a middle ground, and learn the art of conflict resolution. The following tools and techniques will simplify the collection process.

USING THE INFORMATION COLLECTION FORMS

It is recommended that the forms be provided the counselee as a Personal Assessment Form (Homework) where the counselee will have the opportunity to discover things about themselves that they have not considered, addressing the issues for the first time. The Collection Forms are beneficial resources, particularly during the early stages of Christian counseling. This allows the counselor to refer to the information, track the counselee's progress, and discover answers to questions that can help both the counselor and counselee identify possible triggers and find a solution.

Example:

- Obtaining health information (illnesses, medications, drug abuse history)
- Identification data (educational background)
- Health information (illnesses, medications, drug abuse history)
- Religious background (provides information on counselee's denomination, spiritual condition and activities)
- Personality information (describes general emotional and psychological condition)
- Marriage and family information (identifies counselee's support network and family structures)

MAY NEED TO STATE THE TOOLS AGAIN

The Advanced Questioning Form can be used, as a follow-up to those questions originally asked on the Personal Assessment Form will aid the counselee in taking an active role in the discovery process.

There are six areas of personal data that can provide the counselor with vital information and reveal much about the counselee, such as personality, attitudes, and beliefs. When counseling, asking "what" or "how" types of questions will help the counselees to express their feelings reducing the possibility of emotional avoidance. Asking the right questions can provide further opportunity for the counselor to explore the issues at a much deeper level. This ultimately will help both the counselor and counselee to confront the problem, thus leading to a positive outcome.

Student Notes

Lesson 12

Personal Assessment Forms

The Personal Assessment Forms (A model inspired by Dr. Wayne A. Mack) are designed as a counselor resource for discovering the person's emotional makeup and identifying problem patterns. As discussed in the prior chapters of this book, a person's worldview and personality are dictated by their religious and political beliefs and physical health. While collecting personal information may seem intrusive, information gathered can provide critical material that can expose deep-rooted truths and links to a troubled past. Relevant information, such as a person's physical and mental health can be an obstacle to resolving stressful difficulties. For example, a person who has experienced a sudden death of a loved one may suffer a time of deep depression as they mourn their loss. The individual who has suffered a significant loss must take emotional steps to reconcile him or herself to the fact that this is the close of a chapter in the life of the person who is going through this time of significant trauma.

The recovery process takes time does not come with a set deadline for emotional recovery, and the spiritual caregiver must stand ready to provide comfort to the person who is going through this time of emotional suffering. If the person who is suffering the loss is in the same emotional state of mind a year following the death and there are no noticeable signs of recovery, then there may be something much more profound and physical to consider. The spiritual counselor may be equipped to address the person in crisis from a scriptural perspective. However, a person who is rooted in depression for an extended period may be suffering from a chemical imbalance that can only be resolved by medication.

If while interviewing the counselee it is discovered that the individual has not received care from a medical professional, then it may be incumbent of the counselor to recommend the counselee to seek a medical checkup before undergoing a lengthy counseling session. The person who is a suffering chemical imbalance as a result of emotional stress is not crazy but somewhat clouded by a lack of hope. While providing spiritual care is the right passages to recovery, a person who is dealing with a chemical imbalance will be distracted by feelings and a sense of doom. A person's physical condition must first be addressed and corrected before moving on to the next stage of spiritual counseling. The PAF form will help in retrieving crucial information that will not only provide a synopsis of the person's life, but it can also reveal underlying medical issues that can hinder the recovery process.

Information Collection Tools

Now we will look at the tools and techniques that we can employ to help us gather information in an organized and methodical fashion.

PRIMARY TOOLS

(1) Personal Assessment Forms
(2) Advanced Questioning Form (AQF)

The Advanced Questioning Form can be a useful tool in the initial stages of counseling for the following reasons:

- Requiring that counselees complete a PAF indicates a counselor's concern for thoroughness.
- The form provides constant access to basic information that the counselor may forget or neglect to cover during the counseling sessions.

- The information helps to prepare the counselor for the counseling sessions. It will often reveal the initial direction the counseling should take.
- Completing the form help counselees think about the issues that will be discussed.
- Discussing information from the form with the counselee can provide a natural and appropriate entry point into the counseling session.

ADVANCED QUESTIONING FORM (AQF) Sample

The Personal Assessment Forms, Advance Questioning Forms, and Negative Behavioral Patterns Form, designed, and formatted for immediate use and can acquire from Chaplains International, Inc.

EMPLOYMENT AND HEALTH

- How would you describe your health both past and Present?
- How would you describe your pattern of sleep?
- Describe your employment role. If you could change anything about your employment, what changes would be made?
- Have there been any recent changes in your daily routine? I so please describe what changes have taken place.

WHAT IS IMPORTANT IN YOUR LIFE?

- Who are the most important people in your life, in what order, and why?
- Your relationships, share your joy, sadness, disappointment, and heartache.

- When a problem arises, how do you handle the situation?
- Who in your life are you most comfortable with sharing your most private thoughts and why?
- If not your spouse or a family member, how did this relationship begin?
- How important is this person in your life and why?
- How is your relationship with God and where does He fit in to the current situation?
- What steps are you taking strengthen your relationship with God and how is your prayer life?
- Where does church fit into your life, and do you spend time in the Word of God?
- How have you gone about resolving pat problems?
- Describe your greatest strengths, deficiencies, and weaknesses.

EMOTIONAL EXPERIENCES

Emotionally, how do other people see you?

If you could change anything about your life emotionally, what change would you make?

If you could playback a recording of moments in your life, how would you see yourself emotionally?

LOOKING BACK OVER YOUR LIFE

What are your regrets and what would you do to change the past?

As you review the past, what do you see as your greatest accomplishment?

Tell me about your growth as a Christian.

What steps can you take to improve your relationship with Christ?

YOUR PERCEPTION OF EVENTS

- Currently in your life, what do you see as your greatest concern?
- Why has the problem escalated to this level of concern?
- What have you done so far to address this problem?
- How well do you handle constructive criticism and how do you react when confronted? Please explain.
- What does it say about you as a person?
- If criticism is difficult for you handle, explain why and what and what may be the root cause.

HISTORICAL INFORMATION

- What events were taking place in your life when the problem first arose?
- What are the most positive influences in your life and what have been the most negative influences?
- What brings out the worst and the best in you?
- Where do you go and where do you look for security, happiness, fulfillment, comfort, and joy in your life?
- What are your greatest worries and why?
- What in your life gives you the greatest amount of joy?
- How do you see yourself?
- How do you define failure in your life?
- On your deathbed, how would people sum up your life?
- What do you see as your basic rights?
- When you pray what do you pray for and why?
- What do you obsess about the most and how has it affected your life and relationships?
- When you communicate with others do you talk mostly about yourself and why?
- What do you see as your priorities?
- Do you tend to daydream throughout the day? If so, please explain what and why and how it affects your life.

- Do you have trust issues? If so, please explain
- Do you blame God for your failures? If so, please explain

Identifying the Issues

Our worldview is defined as our personal model, theory, assumption, interpretation, and frame of reference for the world around us. It is the way we "see" the world and how it influences our attitudes, thoughts, and leads us to certain choices and behaviors. For example, two people could be looking at the same identical facts, and they would both acknowledge these facts, but each person's interpretation of these facts represents their prior experiences, and the facts have no real meaning whatsoever apart from the interpretation or perception. Negative experiences from certain people, places, and circumstances in our past sow the seeds for the negative thoughts, perception about life, personal feelings, and daily behaviors. By identifying and addressing, the problem at the core provides the steppingstones towards reconciliation.

PRESENTING THE ISSUE

Ask the counselee to answer the following questions on separate sheet of paper.

1. What is the nature of your problem?
2. What have you done thus far to deal with the problem?
3. How long has this been a problem?
4. What motivated you to seek counsel now?
5. What do you hope to gain from the counseling session?
6. How would you describe yourself, what type of person are you?
7. What are your greatest fears?
8. Is there any other information we should know about?

Review of Topic

Our personal interpretation of the world around us ("Our worldview,") dictates our thoughts, feelings perception, attitudes, and behaviors, which affect how we interact with other people and how we deal with problems in our lives. Conditioning results in repeated behavioral patterns sparked by emotional triggers. Working with the person in collecting personal information will create a profile of the individual, which can aid both the counselor and counselee in discovering a solution as well as breaking and replacing bad habits.

NEGATIVE BEHAVIORAL PATTERNS (NBP)

Counselors may use a tool called "Negative Behavioral Patterns" (NBP) Journal Form as a homework assignment for the counselee to complete (For a period of one to four weeks) and to help uncover specific behavioral patterns. For instance, a counselee may be dealing with anger, as mentioned earlier. The counselee should keep an NBP journal to determine the triggers that lead to an emotional outburst. The counselor may discover the person's daily habits may be linked to a time of day, fatigue, use of alcohol, and arguments with friends or family. Gathering such information is useful for discovering a pattern of behavior or habit and its triggers.

Understanding behavioral patterns will benefit both the counselor and counselee and help in charting out a strategy for altering negative behavior, which will result in breaking old habits and avoiding triggers that lead to destructive behavior.

USING RESOURCE MATERIAL

The Negative Behavioral Patterns form, and the Taking Thought Captive Worksheet are two excellent resources that can be given to the counselee as homework assignments that will help them work through behavioral issues. The PAF form helps the counselee discover and document events leading up to specific patterns of behavior so that they can be appropriately addressed.

While some of the techniques and resources recommended in this course of study are designed for use in more control environment, the principles can be utilized when providing peer counseling. For example, if you are on a ride-along with a police officer, and the conversation led to a discussion of a failing marriage, presenting the Personal Assessment Forms and other like resources is not recommended. Unless there is a prior agreement between you and the officer, introducing these forms would create the appearance of a clinician counselee relationship in a setting where there are no parameters. However, asking questions listed on the forms during a casual conversation may prove useful and less invasive.

SAMPLE

NEGITIVE BEHAVIORAL PATTERNS (NBP) FORM

Full Name	Date

Direction: During the course of week document each event that lead to a negative behavioral response. For example did you watch a news broadcast that made you angry causing an emotional outburst or negative feelings? Did your spouse or co-worker say something that ruined your day?

Sunday	Monday	Tuesday	Wednesday	Thursday	Friday	Saturday

Emotions	Check	MORNING - DESCRIBE YOUR EMOTIONS AT THE TIME OF THE INCIDENT
Irritated		
Anger		
Outrage		
Sad		
Depressed		
Emotions		**AFTERNOON - DESCRIBE YOUR EMOTIONS AT THE TIME OF THE INCIDENT**
Irritated		
Anger		
Outrage		
Sad		
Depressed		
Emotions		**EVENING - DESCRIBE YOUR EMOTIONS AT THE TIME OF THE INCIDENT**
Irritated		
Anger		
Outrage		
Sad		
Depressed		

Controlling Your Thoughts Worksheet
Worksheet 3

Name: ______________________________Date: _______

1. What is the thought which is concerning to you that needs to be addressed or changed?

____
____
____
____
____
____
____
____
____
____

2. What are the circumstances that gave rise to the thought that concerns you?

____
____
____
____
____
____
____
____
____
____

3. What is God's truth on this subject(s)? (*Write out verses from your study or the counsel of others.*)

4. What is the concise prayer that you pray when the thought arises? (*thanksgiving and request*)

5. What specific actions will you take concerning your circumstance or thinking?

Student Notes

Lesson 13

Biblical Process of Change

Carnal Feelings vs. God's Will - Our ability of self-awareness helps us determine whether our perceptions are reality-based on principles, or those feelings based on past emotions. We have the freedom to yield to our emotions s or rely on biblical principles set forth by God through His holy word. We must help the people we counsel understand that a person past is always accompanied by a closet full of skeletons. We cannot change the person we used to be. However, we can become the person God wants us to be and the person we should have always been.

In this portion of the lesson, we will present five steps necessary for change, also known as the "Five-R's" of Biblical Change:

A. Responsibility
B. Repentance
C. Reconciliation
D. Renewal of Minds
E. Replacement

There are three (3) major excuses that are widely accepted to explain the nature of man today.

- Genetic– I am the way I am because of my genes. It is the genes I inherited from my family.

- Psychological– My childhood experiences essentially determine my character and personality.
- Environmental– Someone else or something else in my environment (social and economic situations, national law/ policies) is the cause for our behaviors.

Steps towards Repentance

Confessing – There is a two-fold nature of inward confession that is revealed in the meaning of the Greek verb "*homologeo*" ("to say the same thing"). First, we must acknowledge to ourselves and to God the fact that we are sinners. Second, we must agree with God about the nature of our sin.

Choosing – True repentance always includes a willful resolution not to repeat the sin.

Responsibility- Society tells us we are the product of our social surroundings, a worldview that excuses people from responsibility for their thoughts and actions. We cannot deny the power and exposure to social conditioning, however, to say that we are governed by those influences and therefore we must live accordingly is animalistic lessening our humanity and disavowing our God-given duty to choose right from wrong.

Responsible people feel the physical, social, and psychological effects of their actions, and their responses to such stimuli should be Biblically based regardless of their personal feelings. A person may not feel like forgiving the people who have harmed them, but if they are believers in Christ Jesus, they are more likely to subscribe to biblical principles and mandates and forgive their offenders. The irresponsible person yields to their emotions, repeating their actions, and satisfying their fleshly desires without regard for consequences. This person avoids making hard choices and makes excuses for not doing the right thing rationalizing their misgivings.

For some, it is challenging to accept that life's difficulties are often the result of bad decision making, and blaming others allow for these difficulties to remain unresolved. The first step to resolution is to acknowledge that issues exist, the role we play, and the choices made. For example, a child molester may reason that because he was molested as a child, his life as a repeat sex offender stems from his upbringing, thus rejecting the notion of personal responsibility. While a child, molester may rationalize that his abusive past is responsible for his uncontrolled emotions and conduct; in reality, it does not eliminate his responsibility for his actions towards others. As human beings, we are governed by emotions, reasoning, and choice, which lead to either a positive or a negative outcome.

The following graphs can help identify the kind of people we truly are:

Reactive People

- There's nothing I can do.
- That's just the way I am.
- He/she made me so mad.
- They won't allow that.
- I must do that.
- I cannot.
- I must ___________
- If only ___________
- I must ___________

Responsible People

- Let's look at our alternative.
- I can choose a different approach.
- I control my own feelings.
- I can create an effective presentation.
- I choose an appropriate response.
- I chose.
- I prefer ___________
- I will ___________
- I choose to ___________

A serious problem with uncontrolled reactive language is that it becomes self-fulfilling, and negative concepts are reinforced and support faulty thinking. The negative results of their actions produce feelings of victimization, being out of control, and not being in charge of their lives. They blame outside forces, other people, and circumstances, for their situations. As Biblical counselors, we are guided by the Word of God and the principles found within the pages, to instruct (Not condemnation) and help people recognize and take responsibility for their actions.

Repentance - Change begins with honest repentance

✞ The Bible tells us, *"Repent therefore and be converted, that your sins may be blotted out, so that times of refreshing may come from the presence of the Lord" (Acts 3:19)*

The word "repent" (shubin Hebrew) basically means to turn back or turn around. Repentance is a necessary component for genuine change. People who want change must turn from sin, which is the state of self-rule. They surrendered to their flesh and allowed it to dictate their lifestyles. Their actions are motivated by the desire to satisfy their feelings and emotions. The outcome of this lingering disease called "the flesh" is a sin. We can use the following Biblical passage to reflect this point. True repentance requires us to turn to God for forgiveness and renewal.

- ✞ *"Now the works of the flesh are evident, which are: adultery, fornication, uncleanliness, lewdness, idolatry, sorcery, hatred, contentions, jealousies, outbursts of wrath, selfish ambitions, dissentions, heresies, envy, murders, drunkenness, revelries, and the like. (Galatians 5:19-21)*

Elements of true repentance

Comprehending – Before repentance can take place, there must be a willingness to embrace truth and the desire to replace our destructive worldview with biblical principles. The Greek word most often used is translated the English word *"repentance"* is metanoia, which means *"a change of mind."* After a person recognizes their old and sinful ways in the light of the Gospel of Jesus Christ, accept responsibility for their actions, there is a change of behavior and attitudes.

Confessing –There is a two-fold nature of inward confession that is revealed in the meaning of the Greek verb homologeo, which means, "to say the same thing." First, we must acknowledge our sinful nature, second, we must understand our sinful nature considering Scripture. The Bible teaches that if we confess our sins, He (God) is faithful and just to forgive us our sins and to cleanse us from all unrighteousness. (1 John 1:8-9) The Old Testament writer wrote, "He who covers his sins will not prosper, but whoever confesses and forsakes them will have mercy." (Proverbs 28:13)

Effects of true repentance

- ✞ *"For observe this very thing that you sorrowed in a godly manner. What diligence it produced in you, what clearing of yourself, what indignation, what fear, what vehement desire, what zeal, what vindication! In all things you proved yourself to be clear in this matter." (II Corinthians 7: 11)*

Restitution –This word means "to set things right" that is the repentant sinner must fulfill any obligations to the offended party. This includes both an outward confession when it is appropriate and a willingness to accept the consequences of our actions. James tells us,

- ✞ *"Confess your trespasses to one another, and pray for one another, that you may be healed. "(James 5:16) another, that you may be healed. "(James 5:16)*

Regret – True repentance may not always be accompanied by emotions, but in many cases, a feeling of sorrow validates and points to a real change in thinking. Emotional responses alone are not always an indicator of genuine repentance as often seen in the cases of spousal abuse where the perpetrator may express sorrow and regret only to repeat the same offense repeatedly. King David of Israel *(regarding his transgressions with Bathsheba)* demonstrates true repentance for his adulterous behavior and expresses both sorrow and true remorse.

- ✞ *"For I acknowledge my transgressions. And my sin is always before me. Against You, you only, have I sinned, and done this evil in Your sight."* (Psalm 51:3-4)

Reconciliation

When our sin has resulted in a broken relationship with another, true repentance will cause us to do whatever it takes to transform the conflict into a peaceful and edifying friendship. Jesus commanded His followers,

- ✞ *"... be reconciled with your brother, and then come and offer your gift." (Matthews 5:24)*

Reconciliation through forgiveness

What is forgiveness? - The primary Greek verb translated "forgive" (aphiemi) means "to send away" or "to release" or "to pardon." However, forgiveness has also rightly been described as a promise, because when God forgives, He promises that He will never hold our sins against us (Jeremiah 31:34). Therefore, the best definition of forgiveness is a promise of pardon. We need to ask for forgiveness from God and each other for our transgressions.

The forgiveness of God – Man, needs forgiveness from God both before salvation and after salvation. The forgiveness is given before salvation can be called "judicial forgiveness," "because God acted as a judge, declaring us righteous forever and delivering us from eternal condemnation" (Romans 4:3-8). The forgiveness needed after salvation can be called "parental forgiveness" because God is now our loving Father who wants to free us from the discomfort of His chastening (Hebrews 12: 5-11).

Our forgiveness– We are to forgive one another just as God has forgiven us (Ephesians 4:32; Colossians 3:13), so when we grant forgiveness to someone, we are promising that we will "not remember" their sin anymore (Jeremiah 31:34). That means we will never use their sin against them, so practically we are saying the following to the one we forgive: [12]

- "I will not remind you of this sin."
- "I will not mention it to anyone else."
- "I will not allow my mind to dwell on it."

Whom should we forgive? Some passages in scripture imply that we can only forgive those who ask for it (e.g., Luke 17:3-4), while other passages suggest that we should forgive everyone who sins against us, regardless of whether they ask for it or not (e.g., Mark 11:25). How can we understand this discrepancy? Perhaps the best way to understand this is to make a distinction between the "transaction of forgiveness "and the "attitude of forgiveness."

The attitude of forgiveness –The Bible encourages us to reconcile with those who have trespassed against us and settled our differences. When doing so, our attitude should never be one of anger, bitterness, resentment, or ill will. We are called upon to treat those who have offended us with kindness and grace. (Read Romans 12:17-21). We are commanded to loved one everyone (read Luke 6:27-35), so we must desire their best, which means we will do everything we can to bring them to repentance. This loving attitude has been called "forgiveness of the heart." It has also been called "vertical forgiveness" because it is mentioned only in the context of prayer. It is something that we do before God that enables us to have the right attitude toward a person. Jesus says,

✞ *"My heavenly Father also will do to you if each of you, from his heart, does not forgive his brother his trespasses." (Matthew 19:35)*

Any time someone wrongs us, we should pray to God. We can help counselee pray this way:

✞ *"Father, you know what has happened between JOHN and me. Help me to not be angry or bitter towards him/her, nor seek revenge in any way, but help me to love him and desire only what is good in his life. Please work in his heart and bring him to repentance so that we can have a reconciled relationship. Use me in any way You can to help him achieve this goal.*

The transaction of forgiveness –God does not make a blanket promise of a pardon for sin to people unless they are genuinely repentant. Notice what Luke says, "Repent, and let every one of you is baptized in the name of Jesus Christ for the remission of sins. (Acts 2:38) Action on the part of the individual must take place for the transaction to be complete. The prerequisite for real change is an encounter with Jesus Christ.

Further discussion about the five elements to the Biblical process of change

1. Taking responsibility
2. Repentance
3. Reconciliation
4. Renewal of mind
5. Replacement of attitude and thoughts

Taking responsibility - The counselor must instill in the counselee the understanding and need for taking responsibility and having accountability for their actions.

Repentance–Repentance for our sinful thoughts and behavior is necessary in order for genuine change to occur. God does not make the promise of pardon to us unless we are willing to change our way of life. To repent, one must comprehend that our old ways are inconsistent with God's teachings, confess our sinful thoughts and actions; then choose to follow Godly principles. The fruits of repentance are regret, restitution, and reconciliation.

We reconcile through forgiveness

We are to ask for God for forgiveness when we have sinned against Him. When God forgives, He promises that He will never hold our sins against us. God commands us to forgive others. Therefore, forgiveness is a matter of obedience, regardless of how we feel.

Renewal of Mind - We must shift our worldview, the way we see and perceive the events around us. The Bible calls this shift "a renewal of the mind." The "renewal of the mind" can create essential changes in one's life because things are now seen from a biblical perspective. If we are content with minor changes, our lives, we can focus on our attitudes and behaviors and hope for a lasting change. However, if we want to make significant quantum-leap changes, we need to work on shifting from our inaccurate worldview to Biblically based principles. Biblical principles are as solid as a "rock." They are natural laws that cannot be broken. Therefore, it is impossible for us to break the natural Law of God. We can only break ourselves against the Law. While the individual may look at their own lives and interactions in terms of their worldviews or maps emerging from their experiences and conditionings, these maps are not the territory. They are just "subjective reality," only an attempt to describe the territory. The "objective reality," or the territory itself, is composed of the "rock" principles that govern human growth and happiness – God's natural laws that are underpinned every civilized society throughout history and comprise the roots of every family and institution that has endured and prospered. The degree to which our mental maps accurately or inaccurately describe the territory does not alter its existence.

The principles of God

The principles we are referring to are from God, presented in the Bible, and are the foundation of enduring social and ethical systems. They are self-evident and can easily be validated by any individual. They are part of the human condition, consciousness, and conscience. They exist in all human beings. These are principles of fairness, integrity, honesty, human dignity, service, quality, excellence, potential, growth, patience, nurturance, love, and encouragement.[13]

When we value correct principles, we have truth and knowledge of things as they are and should be. The more closely our maps or worldviews are aligned with God's principles or natural laws; the more accurate and functional they will be. Correct maps will infinitely influence our personal and interpersonal effectiveness far more than any amount of effort expended on just changing our attitudes and behaviors.

The prerequisite of renewal -Prior to the "renewal of the mind" experience, our mind is corrupt, blinded, futile, and darkened. The Bible says,

- ✞ *"They did not like to retain God in their knowledge..." (Romans 1:28)*
- ✞ *"Whose minds the gods of this age have blinded, who do not believe, lest the light of the gospel of the glory of Christ, who is image of God, should shine on them..." (2 Corinthians 4:4)*
- ✞ *"...the non-believers walk in the futility of their mind, having their understanding darkened, being alienated from the life of God, because of the ignorance that is in them, because of the blindness of their hearts." (Ephesians 4:17, 18)*

REPLACEMENT

As biblical counselors, it is our responsibility to help the person achieve a change in attitude and actions that is, changing the way they react to life's stressors and emotions, and making biblically based decisions. It requires self-control and addressing difficulties with the mindset of Christ. The Apostle Paul encourages the Ephesians Congregation to replace bad behavior with good and warns them not to grieve the Holy Spirit.

✞ *"Let him who stole steal no longer, but rather let him labor, working with his hands what is good, that he may have something to give him who has need. Let no corrupt word proceed out of your mouth, but what is good for necessary edification, that it may impart grace to the hearers. And do not grieve the Holy Spirit of God, by whom you were sealed for the day of redemption. Let all bitterness, wrath, anger, clamor, and evil speaking be put away from you, with all malice. And is kind to one another, tenderhearted, forgiving one another, even as God in Christ forgave you." (Ephesians 4:22-32)*

The concept of replacement - Ephesians chapter four verses 22-24 tell us that we are to change our former way of conduct, the "old man" and describes it as corrupt, requiring a renewal of the spirit. Verse 24 concludes, "…put on the new man which was created according to God, in true righteousness and holiness."

The characteristics of replacement are:

- Breaking of old habits and replacing them with new and wholesome habits.
- Enduring in obedience to God and being willing to fight for change.
- We must restructure our environment in order to remove those things that prohibit change to occur.

"Put on the Lord Jesus Christ and make no provision for the flesh in regard to its lusts." (Romans 13:14)

Maintaining Change / The garden analogy

Positive changes are often short-lived, leaving the person feeling hopeless and frustrated. The final step in the rehabilitative process is maintaining personal change. We will use the analogy of a garden to represent this process of maintaining change.

- The garden represents our lives
- Weather conditions represent external circumstances and difficulties, which we have no control over.
- Seeds represent our thoughts, and the plants are our actions
- Trees represent our character
- Fruits and flowers are a product of our character
- Weeds, wild plants, wild trees, and poisonous fruits represent negative thoughts, and actions
- The counselees are the assigned caretakers
- The counselors are gardening advisors
- God is the Master Gardener

Our choices will dictate whether our garden will be consumed by weeds, wild and vegetation, or a beautifully tended garden with fragrant flowers and trees bearing fruit. A Biblical approach to counseling offers new opportunities to those who are struggling to maintain their gardens by assisting them in their journey to emotional enrichment and spiritual renewal. Often what we have discovered during the counseling process is a garden in disarray, a garden being robbed of vital nutrients that are stifling growth and productivity.

OVERCOMING FAULTY THINKING

The first step in personal growth is to help the person examine their cognitive thought process as it relates to their situation and evaluate whether those thoughts and beliefs are based on truth or based on the disarray of emotions, lies, and misconceptions. A faulty cognitive thought process leads to negative beliefs that contribute to a dysfunctional perception of events.

📖 Freeman et al. (1991) state that *"One of the major premises of cognitive view of human functioning is that automatic thoughts shape both individual's emotions and their actions in response to events" (p.4). "a second premise of cognitive therapy is that an individual's beliefs, assumptions, and schemas shape the perception and interpretation of events" (p.4).*

Biblically counseling can lead to a renewal of the mind and promote change in a person's life, but it cannot eliminate their past pain and suffering or remove all difficulties resulting from their dysfunctional past. Breaking old habits can take a lifetime of effort, learning to exercise self-control and begins with a change in thought patterns. In our studies, we have discussed the topic of personal responsibility, taking action for our destructive thoughts and behavior by confessing our sins and failures to Almighty God, and seeking reconciliation and renewal. We can promote emotional and spiritual awareness in the person as it pertains to the sins of the heart (hidden thoughts, attitudes, and motivations) as well as behavioral sins that are seen manifested in words and actions.

Next, we must help the person set goals for the future using a biblical framework and principles followed by a plan of action. In this portion of our lesson, it is our goal as Christian counselors to help and encourage the person who is seeking real change in their lives to commit to a plan of action, one that will lead to a permanent change in thought and lifestyle. We must help the counselee to draw closer to a concept that includes a plan of action, introducing them to a platform of thinking that uses the acronym "ACCEPT" as a basic model.

Example

A – Acknowledge responsibility for our thoughts and actions.
C – Choose to live by biblical principles in all circumstances
C – Commit to a plan of eliminating whatever hinders biblical change

E – Execute plan and set new goals.
P – Persevere in faithful obedience to Biblical principles
T – Trust God for the strength and resources for change.

True change in one's life requires a renewal of the mind and spirit and takes an abundance of time and energy, which is not always an easy process.

Noted author Chris Thurman Ph.D. in his book,

📖 *"The Lies We Believe"* puts it this way, *(Paraphrased text) "Our brain is like a processing center with access to a personal Library of thousands of pieces of recorded information ready to access at a moment's notice. These recordings contain beliefs, attitudes, and expectations that have been processed during our lifetime. Some recorded information bares a modicum of truth while other sources of information are based on lies. Our emotional and spiritual wellbeing hinges on the annals of information which sets the fourth the foundation for our actions and response to the challenges of life."*

ALLEGORICAL TRUTHS

One Biblical truth is *we reap what we have sown* or in modern terms refer to as cause and effect. That is, we take responsibility for our thoughts and actions. The following are some allegorical truths that put things into perspective.

- THOUGHT (Seed) If we sow a thought (seed) and we reap an action (plant)
- ACTION (Plant) If we sow an action (plant) and we reap a habit (tree)
- HABIT (Tree) If we sow a habit (tree) and we reap a character (fruit)

- CHARACTER (Fruit) If we sow a character (fruit) and we reap a destiny (garden)
- DESTINY (Could be a garden or a jungle depends on what we sow)

PLAN OF ACTION

Choose Biblical viewpoint in all circumstances

We need to reach out to the people we counsel, help them to understand that spiritual change involves personal choice, that is to either act on personal feelings (according to the flesh) or bases our actions on what is taught by the Word of God. The principles of God Almighty must become our most treasured standard by which we base our thoughts and actions in order for us to find renewal and reconciliation.

- ✞ *"But seek first the kingdom of God and His righteousness, and all these things shall be added to you" (Matthew 6:33)*

Establishing and maintaining a personal relationship with God is a sacred journey on the part of everyone. As ministers Gospel and Biblical counselors, it is our job to help the person along his or her journey, to discover a deeper, more meaningful, and personal relationship with the creator of the universe. As counselors, we should never presume that it is our place to interfere with the process. We must guide the counselee to pray, asking God to reveal His wisdom.

- ✞ *"For the LORD gives wisdom; from His mouth come knowledge and understanding." (Proverbs 2:3-8)*
- ✞ *"If any of you lacks wisdom, let him ask of God, who gives to all liberally and without reproach, and it will be given to him." (James 1:5)*

Counselees should give themselves entirely to knowing God's will and purpose by spending time studying the Scriptures and gaining wisdom. The deeper our understanding, the greater the opportunity to make decisions that are consistent with the principles of truth found in God's Word.

- ✝ *"Show me the path where I should walk, O Lord; point out the right road for me to follow." (Psalm 25:4)*

Commit to a plan to eliminate whatever hinders biblical change

Life is full of distractions and temptations that can interfere with and hinder spiritual growth. In a growing society where there are many distractions, we find ourselves plagued with violence, promiscuity, drugs, alcohol, and political mayhem that overwhelm our minds. As children of God, each person must look within him or herself, identify what distractions most interfere with their relationship with God, and set boundaries.

We can help people learn to be cognizant of spiritual risks that set the stage for sin by teaching them to be aware of their surroundings and avoid societal influences and emotional triggers that lead to temptation and spiritual failure.

- ✝ *"Let us go up to the mountain of the Lord, He will teach us His ways and we shall walk in His paths." (Isaiah 2:3)*
- ✝ *"Commit your works to the Lord, and your thoughts will be established." (Proverbs 16:3)*

The counselor can suggest to the counselee to make a list of people, places, books, music, magazines, websites, and activities that would promote sinful thoughts, desires, and behaviors to be aware in the event of unforeseen situations. If possible, the counselor may establish a mentorship program at a local church where the counselee can reach out to someone mature in their faith, a person who can provide counsel and support during moments of stress and temptation.

Study the Bible daily - A daily habit of studying the Word of God will not only encourage a person in their daily walk but will also strengthen them spiritually against spiritual attacks cast by the enemy.

Journaling - Journaling has been a technique used in both in the Christian and secular counseling arena and is useful for personal documentation of a person's emotions, feelings, and habits which allows the individual to observe their lives in real-time giving them the option to make changes and take extra precaution when deemed necessary.

Realistic goals -The plan should include achievable goals, specific in its actions, measurable in its results, following a structured timeline. Nouthetic Counseling. Dr. Jay Adams is the founder of the Nouthetic Counseling Movement, a counseling technique that teaches that the answers to the stress and difficulties of life are anchored in biblical truth and theology and that the Bible is the foundation and source for all counseling needs. Therefore, we should encourage the counselee to use the Word of God as a platform for spiritual renewal and personal change.

Scriptural encouragement

- ✞ *"Whatever you do, do it heartily, as to the Lord and not to men, knowing that from the Lord you will receive the reward of the inheritance; for you serve the Lord Christ." (Colossians 3:23-24)*

Encourage the counselee that God works in the lives of those who are faithful. "*He (God) who has begun the good work in you will complete it the day of Christ Jesus.*" *(Philippians 1:6)*

Encourage the counselee that he or she can achieve all of their goals if they rely on the strength of Jesus Christ and not their own. "*I can do all things through Christ who strengthens me.*" *(Philippians 4:13)*

Encourage the counselee to continue to persevere in faithful obedience to Biblical principles.

- ✞ "*Let us not grow weary while doing good, for in due season we shall reap if we do not loose heart. Therefore, as we have opportunity, let us do good to all.*" (*Galatians 6:9-10)*

Habits are powerful factors in people's lives because they are consistent, often unconscious patterns, they daily, express our character, and contribute to our effectiveness or ineffectiveness. In the process of change, results may not be readily apparent, and our impatience sometimes gets the better of us, causes us to lose heart before we can experience true transformation. The Bible refers to bad habits (bad behavior) as "strongholds" of the enemy, (meaning Satan) a form of spiritual warfare that takes place between our flesh and our spirit.

- ✞ "*For though we walk in the flesh, we do not war according to the flesh. For the weapons of our warfare are not carnal but the might in God for pulling down strongholds, casting down arguments and every things that exalts itself against the knowledge of God, bringing every thought into captivity to the obedience of Christ.*"*(2 Corinthians 10:3-6)*
- ✞ "*Reject profane and old wives' fables and exercise yourself toward godliness. For bodily exercise profits a little, but godliness is profitable for all things, having promise of the life that now is and of that which is to come.*" *(1 Timothy 4:7-9)*

HOW DO WE DEVELOP PERSEVERANCE IN OUR LIVES?

It has been said that "A thousand-mile journey starts with the first step," and as Christian Counselors, we should encourage people to follow Jesus each step of the way, in every situation, moment by moment, one day at a time. We must allow Jesus to lead us and guide our hearts and minds in order to experience a true transformation of our souls.

Perseverance is obeying God and submitting to the will even when things do not seem to make sense or produce results as we expect. The Bible teaches the principle of obedience as seen in the scenario found in Joshua 6:1-20 when God instructs Joshua to overtake the city of Jericho and commands him and his army to march around Jericho once each day for six days. Conventional wisdom says in order for us to defeat our enemies, we should prepare for battle and pray for God to protect and guide our efforts, as would be the ordinary course of action. However, in the case of Jericho God had other plans in which Joshua was required to persevere in the Lord, follow His instructions, and blow the trumpets as the Hebrew army marched around the walls of the city in order to experience victory. This required three things to take place on Joshua's part,

1. Rather than rely upon conventional wisdom Joshua obeyed God (Obedience)
2. Joshua trusted God that His decision was correct despite any concern he may have had at the time (Trust)
3. Joshua understood that whatever the outcome of events, God was in control (God is in control)

The Bible teaches us to rely upon God through perseverance so that we may build good character and dependence upon Him in all things.

- ✝ *"We also glory in tribulation knowing that tribulation produces perseverance, character; and character, hope." (Romans 5:3-4)*

The key to perseverance for the believers is having a clear view of the goal and complete it.

- ✝ *"And in this I give advice: It is to your advantage not only to be doing what you began and desired to do a year ago; but now you also must complete doing it; that as there was a readiness to desire it, so there also may be a completion out of what you have." (2 Corinthians 8:10-11)*

Our ability to persevere helps us to strengthen our faith in God. The Christian life begins with faith but grows through perseverance.

- ✝ *"But also, for this reason, giving all diligence, add to your faith virtue, to virtue knowledge, to knowledge self-control, to self-control perseverance, to perseverance godliness, to godliness to brotherly kindness, and to brotherly kindness love. For if these things are yours and abound, you will be neither barren nor unfruitful in the knowledge of our Lord Jesus Christ." (2 Peter 1:5-8)*

How can we keep going when we feel like quitting?

There are times life when emotionally, we feel like giving up and throwing in the towel when it seems that things are not moving in the right direction, and God is silent to our prayers. We can avoid discouragement by keeping our eyes on the goal set by God through His holy Word and seek the rewards of heaven, not things of this world.

- ✝ *"My brethren, count it for joy when you fall into various trials, knowing that the testing of your faith produces patience. But let patience have its perfect work, that you may be perfect and complete, lacking nothing." (James 1:2-4)*

Paul exhorts us to fight a good fight, finish the race, and remain faithful to plan God gives us.

- ✝ *I have fought a good fight, I have finished the race, and I have kept the faith. Finally, there laid up for me the crown of righteousness, which the Lord, the righteous Judge, will give to me on that Day, and not to me only but to all who have loved His appearing. (2 Timothy 4:7-8)*
- ✝ Jesus promises us that, *"He who endures to the end will be saved." (Matthew 10:22)*

What does it mean to trust God?

We must recognize that God is trustworthy in all circumstances and situations, that may occur, and we must place our trust in Him above all else regardless of the outcome of events. Trusting God also means obeying His commands even when we do not feel like it or fully understand His reasons or His choices. The Bible provides many examples of this principle of trust. As we explore the Book of Genesis 6:5-22, it teaches that Noah trusted God, when commanded to build a boat in the middle of nowhere for him and his family. While people in the community referred to Noah as a fool, he trusted God and obeyed His command. By doing so, Noah's family was saved from the catastrophic flood that wiped out mankind. In the Book of Psalms, we are reminded by the words of David,

- ✝ *"Blessed is the man who fears the LORD, who delights greatly in His commandments." (Psalm 112:1)*

Prophet Isaiah clearly affirms this principle of trusting in God when he praised God.

- ✞ *"You will keep him in perfect peace, whose mind is stayed on You (God), because he trusts in You (God)." (Isaiah 26:3)*

Plan for change can be frightening, but when the plans are from God, we can rest assured that we can expect something marvelous.

- ✞ *"The Lord will perfect that which concerns me" (Psalm 138:8)*

God definitely wants to help us follow the path that will be most pleasing to Him, not the path that may be most pleasing to us. God instructs us in His Word,

- ✞ *"I will instruct you and teach you in the way you should go; I will guide you with My eye." (Psalm 32:8)*

We can trust in God to work through us even through traumatic and unpredictable events, or seemingly unfair changes in our lives. The Bible teaches, *"And we know that all things work together for good to those who love God, to those who are the called according to His purpose." (Romans 8:28)*

Student Notes

Part 5

Crisis Intervention a Ministry of Presence

Lesson 14

Critical Situational Stress

What is Critical Situational Stress? - Critical Incident Stress Debriefing (CISD) is a technique designed to minimize the impact of major and traumatic events and aid in and emotional recovery. Dr. Jeffrey T. Mitchell, of the University of Maryland, developed the "Critical Incident Stress Debriefing" model to those who work in high-risk occupations. Initially developed for the military, the program was later adopted by law enforcement and emergency service agencies to address the effects of trauma experienced by department personnel during community emergencies, and natural disasters.

Critical Situational Stress is best described as a normal reaction experienced by normal people, as a result of a highly abnormal event. If not adequately addressed, Critical Situational Stress can develop into a critical level of emotional trauma. Life can dish out many unexpected events that can cause severe emotional trauma, for example, the news of a death of a family member, a tragic accident involving a friend, or learning of a personal terminal illness. In cases of severe depression as a result of a traumatic event, referral to healthcare professional would be in order. Normally, an organized debriefing would not take place within the first 24 to 48 hours of the event, allowing time for the crisis to settle and the process of emotions to take place.

Major losses

- Recent divorce or separation
- Financial loss,
- Loss of employment
- Sudden death
- Death due to long term illness
- Suicides

The four-phase process of crisis counseling outline

1. During a crisis, the goal is to minimize the effects of acute stress symptoms by providing emotional and physical support to those who are in crisis and identify those who need to be referred to a mental health professional for further diagnosis.

   Example

   - Providing a ministry of presence
   - Recognizing the gravity of the event
   - Allowing a place to debrief
   - Provide resources and educate
   - Helping them with their family members, i.e., children

2. Assist the person through the normal recovery process by helping them succeed through the FOUR PHASE'S PROCESS of dealing with major loss and stress.

Phase 1 – Accept the reality that there has been a tragedy or loss
Phase 2 – Allow the person to experience the pain of loss resulting from the event
Phase 3 – Adjust to the new environment after the loss by making changes
Phase 4 – Move on with life

PREPARATORY CHECKLIST FOR DEBRIEFING

Emotional trauma can affect people differently, and not all trauma cases are the same. How people deal with a crisis is often related to a person's emotional upbringing, exposure to real-world crisis events, whether the crisis is mild, moderate, or severe, dealing with terminal illness and death.

Dr. Norman Wright in his book "Crisis & Trauma Counseling" *made the following observation, "At one time, 75 percent of the general population in our country have been exposed to some event that meets the criteria of trauma. Now it's even higher. The good news is that only about 25 percent of those exposed to such events become traumatized."*

Since the events of 911, many crisis-counseling models have surfaced; however, the Mitchell approach is used by emergency services than any other model. The debriefing program utilizes a seven-phase process, concepts that can be applied one on one or most common, facilitated in a group setting.

THE DEBRIEFING PROCESS/ CRISIS SITUATIONAL STRESS

<u>One - Introduction Phase</u>

You will want to begin the session by introducing yourself as a member of the crisis team from your church or ministry and explain what your role will be during the debriefing process. You will want to gain the trust of those in attendance, establish ground rules for the sessions, and assure all in who are in attendance of the rules surrounding confidentiality. Let those who are participating know that the debriefing process is not a form of psychotherapy but rather a place where people can vent and share their experience. While it is vital to encourage mutual support and group participation, participants are not required to speak. Some people in attendance may or may not be religious, and questions about their faith and spirituality may not be applicable. Phase two, the fact-finding phase provides a sample of questions you may ask during a debriefing process.

Two - Fact-Finding Phase

The fact-finding phase addresses the "who, what, when why and how." This allows participants to describe the event from their perspective and share their immediate reaction to the crisis. This is known as the reaction stage.

Ask about the crisis

- *"How were you notified?"*
- *"How did you hear about it?*
- *"Where were you?"*
- *"What role did you play in the event?"*

Three - Gathering Thoughts Phase

The gathering thoughts phase is an analysis and discussion of information gained from the fact-finding phase, designed to address the thought process amidst a major crisis and allows the participant to share their story and vent. The following is an example of questions that can be asked during a debriefing session.

- *"What were your first thoughts?"*
- *"What was going on in your mind at that moment?"*
- *"What was your immediate concern?"*

Four - Understanding Reactions Phase

The reaction phase is where emotional trauma is normalized and legitimized, where the most traumatic parts of the experienced are discussed and validated as a normal reaction to an abnormal event.

- *"What part of this crisis bothered you the most?"*
- *"As you look back over what happened, what part of the crisis stood out the most?"*
- *"What would you do different?"*

Five - Identifying Symptoms Phase

This portion of the debriefing model addresses the cognitive aspects of the event and helps the person identify the impact the event has taken both emotionally and physically.

- *How has this affected you?*
- *What was it like for you during the first days after the event?*
- *What was it like for your family members, children?*
- *How has this affected your personal and your family relationship?*

Six - Teaching Phase

The educational portion of the debriefing process, also referred to as the "teaching phase" addresses the emotional aftermath and symptoms that often accompany a catastrophic event. People may experience a variety of cognitive, emotional, behavioral, and physical reactions, days, weeks, months, and even years after a traumatic event has occurred. By recognizing, the possibility of post-traumatic stress after a life-changing event will help the person to put their emotions into proper perspective. Dr. Norman Wright, in his book, Crisis & Trauma Counseling, provides an extensive list of emotional concerns to be aware of and is an invaluable resource for every Christian counselor. The following is a short list of symptoms that people may experience. Counselors can reassure the person or group that the effects of critical situational stress are completely normal. If over some time, the person's emotional or physical symptoms worsen, additional intervention by a medical or mental health professional may be warranted.

When interacting with counselees in crisis we may notice the following symptoms

Tension – physical and emotional tension, muscle tremors or twitches, and restlessness

Fatigue – decreased energy

Sleep disturbances– insomnia, bad dreams, or nightmares

Diet – change in eating or drinking habits

Nausea – nausea, vomiting other gastrointestinal problems

Recurring feelings

- Sadness
- Helplessness
- Anxiety
- Anger
- Discouragement
- Frustration
- Vulnerability
- Depression
- Guilt
- Self-blame
- Insensitivity
- Blaming others

Spiritual Reactions

- Question belief systems and a decrease in spiritual activities
- Question good vs. evil "Why did God allow this to happen?
- Question one's own values
- Angry at God
- Abandon spiritual beliefs and blame God
- Spiritual isolation from others Loss faith in God
- Overcompensation to spiritual beliefs

Stress - Management Principles

The following are some basic stress management principles that have been shown to help reduce the symptoms of severe situational stress.

- Eat nutritious foods: fresh fruits, vegetables and balanced meals
- Get some physical exercise to reduce some of the physiological effects of stress
- Moderate intake of caffeine
- Avoid alcohol or other depressants
- Rest well by getting adequate sleep (at least 8 hours per night)
- Engage in relaxing activities such as walking, stretching, listening to music
- Find time to do things the counselees enjoy such as hobbies, play musical instrument, gardening, etc.
- Avoid changes in counselees daily routines
- Do not make any significant life altering decisions while still stress
- Find friends or a support source to talk to about the incident.
- If the symptoms of stress do not lessen, seek additional intervention.

Seven - Re-Entry Phase

The re-entry phase is a re-cap of conversations and events shared through all phases of the discussion during the debriefing process. At this point, resources and handouts should be made available to those are in attendance, material which can generally be obtained at any local metal health agency or private organization. This portion of our studies is a brief overview, an introduction to the practice of Critical Incident Stress Debriefing. Whether you are a chaplain or pastor, you will want to explore in more detail the CISD model by contacting the International Critical Incident Stress Foundation for more information about training seminars held in your area.

Student Notes

Lesson 15

Traumatic Stress Reactions and Children

Most mental health professionals agree that for the most part, people who suffer personal trauma eventually adapt to their loss and circumstances. In general, young children follow a similar reactive pattern when it comes to a catastrophic event. Children tend to move between three basic postures when a crisis occurs. 1) Children will often show signs of emotional distress days or months after experiencing a tragic event. 2) Children may shut down their emotions. 3) It is not uncommon for children to emotionally withdrawal after a tragedy. Some children may return to normal activities while seemingly oblivious to the situation. Unlike adults, children can only accept as much as they can process cognitively and emotionally. Adults attempting to talk to children about a tragic event may be met with mixed emotions. Children may stare blankly, walk away, change the subject, or act out. They may appear to be in denial. Younger children tend to exhibit clinging behavior and separation anxiety following traumatic stress.

When a traumatic event takes place, children tend to exhibit signs of anger, depression, anxiety, and insecurity that may have a lasting effect well into their adult years. Children do not have the same cognitive level of dealing with trauma as an adult or the ability to draw upon life their experience. Children may detach themselves from reality, acting out their emotions by fantasizing, playing games, oblivious to the fact that a tragedy has occurred. Children reactions sometimes parallel those of adults, with the exception that they reflect adolescent developmental issues. One minute they may discuss the incident with the appropriate expression of feelings, the next day, they may act out childishly. One moment they may want to be near their parents, another moment they may be caught up in an outburst of peer-group hysteria. The more serious the trauma, the more the child may exhibit symptoms of stress and withdrawal. The nearness of the incident may affect the child, whether it is an event that they were personally involved in or an event that a parent or family member experienced. Many of these reactions are a form of Acute Stress Response (ASR).

Key Points to Remember When Dealing with Children's Grief

In general, children grieve when they experience a significant loss in their lives and may express their grief in many ways because of their age and their cognitive ability to deal with a bad situation. Other factors to consider are their cultural and family environment, which may play a role in how they address life-changing events. By identifying, the stress signals that children exhibit during a crisis, we can better assist them through the recovery process.

The goal of crisis counseling involving children

- To assist the child through the normal recovery process
- To identify those children who need a referral to mental health professional
- Not to provide psychotherapy

Children / Post Crisis Behaviors

A child's classification of cognitive development often determines their patterns of response to a traumatic situation. The following outline of behavioral patterns is useful for determining a child's level of emotional understanding.

Pre-School To Kindergarten

WITHDRAWAL - Children may become unusually withdrawn, seemingly detached from reality and withdraw into a state of denial, pretending that a crisis does not exist.

THEMATIC PLAY -Children may act out their emotions by re-enacting certain aspects of the crisis. For example, a child who has witnessed a parental suicided by use of a weapon may role-play, reenacting the event.

ANXIOUS ATTACHMENT - Behavior may include Separation anxiety and showing

- Signs of stress around strangers
- Clinging to parents
- Tantrums

SPECIFIC FEARS -Some fears that are common in children and young adolescents may include the following list.

- Fear of new situations (Unable to move forward in life)
- Unhealthy fear of the unknown
- Fear of males (May be related to abuse)
- Fears of confined spaces
- Fear of violence (Such as domestic violence)

REGRESSION –Young adolescents may show signs of regression in behavior, reflecting an age of innocence before any traumatic event.

School Age Children

PERFORMANCE DECLINE –A noticeable decline in scholastic performance can occur in children and adolescents following a traumatic event.

COMPENSATORY BEHAVIORS -These behaviors may include but not limited to,

- Emotional denial
- Wanting retribution
- Fantasying or acting out (Dissociative Behavior)

MOOD SWINGS - Children may express inappropriate behavior, which may be a sign of avoidance by the child to accept the reality of recent traumatic events.

PSYCHOSOMATIC COMPLAINTS– physical complaints are common symptoms of psychological distress.

- Stomachaches
- Headaches
- Physical aches and pains

Adolescent Age

Acting out Behaviors - They often act out their distress in ways which are ultimately self-destructive. These can include isolation, truancy, drugs and alcohol abuse, hypersexual activity, violence, delinquency, running away, talking about suicide or suicide attempts.

LOW SELF-ESTEEM AND SELF-CRITICISM – Adolescents may blame themselves for the event and express anger over their inability their exercise control over the situation.

DISPLACED ANGER- Adolescents may be unable to deal with their loss or unequipped to control their emotions.

WAYS PARENTS CAN HELP THEIR CHILDREN BE HONEST

WHEN SPEAKING WITH A CHILD - Provide simple answers to their questions. If you do not know the answer to a specific question, be honest with the child.

ALLOW THEM EXPRESS THEIR FEELINGS -Let the child know that it is acceptable to feel sadness, anger, or confusion. Help them to understand that these feelings are natural during the grieving process and speak openly about good or bad memories.

LISTEN to what the child is saying and how they say it. Repeating the child's words and recognizing their fear, anxiety, and insecurity is helpful in the recovery process.

OBSERVE children at play and pay particular attention to what your children are saying when they do play. Children may express feelings of fear or anger more openly while playing with their dolls, action figures, or imaginary friends.

REASSURE the child that you will be there for them, and you will take care of them. Reassure them that they will be safe and not be abandoned.

PHYSICAL PRESENCE –

- Spend extra time with the child
- Leave a night light on if necessary
- Hold your child

Touch is important in giving comfort to children during this period.

REMEDIES FOR STRESS SYMPTOMS -Teach the child that their physical reactions and symptoms such as insomnia, head, and body aches are normal during grieving.

Student Notes

Lesson 16

Grief and Bereavement

Response to loss - During our lifetime, we will all experience some form of bereavement, resulting from the death of a friend or a loved one, loss of a family pet, or dealing with the stages of death and dying of those who are facing a terminal illness. Taking control over grief is a process that takes time and has no set timetable for full or partial recovery. Religious, cultural, and societal influences may play a role in a person's reaction to death and dying and their ability to cope with the immediate or imminent tragedy. The symptoms of death, dying, and loss is often the feeling of shock, emotional numbness, a sense of disbelief, and denial. Often during the loss of a loved one, one person assumes the role of the caregiver and comforter to family and friends giving the appearance of strength stability.

Many years ago, when my grandfather passed away, my grandmother appeared as a pillar of strength. My grandparents had been married for more than 60 years, so it seemed odd to me that I never saw my grandmother grieve since I knew that my grandparents very close. I asked my grandmother why she never grieved the loss of my grandfather, and she said something very profound and something that I never forgot. *"who said that I never grieved the loss of your grandfather? We were married for more than 60 years, and no one can just sweep that away overnight. I grieve the loss of your grandfather every night in the quiet of my memories.* "My grandmother went on to explain that she rarely expressed her emotions publicly as she considered it something very personal and private. While many people openly grieve their losses, a lack of emotional expression is not an indicator of a lack of trauma, and the counselor must extremely careful not to minimize a person perceived lack of grief as a lack of care or concern.

Grief comes in waves, and there may be moments when the person feels a sudden surge of anxiety that affects their inability to perform simple and daily routines. During the grieving process, the person may experience manic-depressive behavior that may affect their cognitive ability to cope with the loss. During the bereavement process, insomnia may occur, or the person may experience restlessness, hyperactivity in which case a referral to a medical professional is in order. Pathological grief usually is often associated with a relationship that is dependent on one central figure, such as spouse or friend.

Definitions, a quick checklist

Grief is the normal emotional response to a crisis where the person has experienced a personal loss. It is unique to the individual who is experiencing the loss, and there is no timetable for completing the grieving process.

Mourning – The expression of grief and is conducted in public as well as in private. The process of mourning takes place in stages.

Bereavement –The term Bereavement is derived from the Old English word ***"berafian"*** *meaning, "to rob"*, and describes the act of mourning.

Anticipatory grief occurs during the process of death and dying. Most notable are patience, family members and medical personnel who are in a hospice care community

Reactions to Grief

The expression of grief is neither an illness nor a disease that requires a diagnoses, treatment, or remedy. Rather it is an emotional reaction (Emotional stress) to an abnormal situation. Grief often produces unusual and extreme behaviors depending on the person's cognitive ability to deal with their current situation. There will be a time in all of our lives when we will experience a major loss and go through the process of grief, and each person will grieve in their own way. As counselors, we must help the person understand the process of grief and reassure them that it is a normal and healthy behavior during such circumstances, though not all following behaviors mentioned are necessarily healthy and may need to be addressed accordingly if they persist.

Acute Reactions

1. Feeling of numbness
2. Reluctance to meet new people
3. Fearful of being alone
4. Afraid to leave the house or fearful of staying in the house
5. Afraid to go to sleep

Physical reactions include

- Tightness in the throat
- Lack of motivation
- Lack of energy to complete common tasks or to finish projects

Other noticeable reactions

- ✓ Angry that no one seems to understand what the person is going through

- ✓ Angry that people expecting the survivor to "get on with life"
- ✓ Wanting to punish someone or damage something for the pain suffering
- ✓ Feelings of Irritability over small things
- ✓ Unpredictable and uncontrollable weeping
- ✓ Unable to find consolation in faith Inability to carry on a normal conversation
- ✓ Unable to sleep without medication or sleeping all the time
- ✓ Unable to make decisions or to solve common problems
- ✓ Unable to concentrate or remember things Impaired judgment Experience panic attacks
- ✓ Wanting to talk about the deceased but fearful of rejection
- ✓ Wearing clothing, jewelry, or other personal items of the deceased
- ✓ Taking on a lot of the deceased's behavior
- ✓ Feel unbearable loneliness Increase in the use of alcohol and/or prescription drugs to ease the pain.
- ✓ Driving too fast or other reckless behaviors
- ✓ Screaming for no apparent reason

Chronic Reactions

- ✓ Loss of hopes and dreams
- ✓ New events trigger old losses
- ✓ Recurring grief during holidays, anniversaries, and birthdays
- ✓ Reluctance to start new relationships

The time that it takes for a person to grieve a personal loss will often depend on how the person died.

For example,

- Was the death sudden or was it a natural death?

- Had the person been fighting a terminal illness or was the death related to a violent crime?
- Were there any unresolved issues between the person who is grieving and the deceased?

The experience of grief is a journey into charted territory and can be a challenge to navigate and a frightening experience. There is the sense of loneliness and despair, the seeming inability to cope. By helping the person learn to manage their emotions and grief, the individual can better embrace the future and realization that recovery is possible. As counselors, we must encourage people to live in the moment and embrace the people in their lives; by doing so, life will become more meaningful.

When to Make a Referral

Every so often, a counselee may come to us with an issue that requires immediate attention or a prompt referral to a healthcare professional (e.g., a psychiatrist, psychologist, or medical doctor).

When it is time to make the call

The following are some of the crises that counselors may need to refer to a mental health professional.

Severe Clinical Depression

Verbalized threats of suicide require emergency intervention by a healthcare professional. Never ignore people who threaten to kill themselves.

Mental Breakdown

Mental breakdowns may exceed the experience of the spiritual counselor and may require a referral to healthcare professionals.

Bizarre Behavior

Bizarre Behavior may be a sign of mental illness and may require immediate medical and psychological attention. Counselors should not assign a psychological diagnosis to the counselee (e.g., psychosis, schizophrenia), unless they are trained psychology professional.

Our Goal in Helping People

Our goals as counselors are simple, and they help to create a framework within which Biblical counseling can operate. Seeing problems from a Biblical perspective helps us understand how God views these issues. Seeing things through God's eyes helps us choose to accept His way of resolving problems.

Lesson 17

Preparing for Approaching Death

When a person enters the final stage of the dying process, there are different dynamics at work. There are Physical changes that take place as the body starts to shut down. During this stage, the patient is made as comfortable as possible. The other dynamics of the death process include the emotional, spiritual, and mental aspects of dying.

When we go through the process of stages of dying, our "spirit" begins the final process of release from the body, its immediate environment, and all attachments. This release may depend on resolving unfinished issues and receiving permission to "let go" from family members. These "events" are natural in the spiritual preparation to move from this existence to the next dimension. The most appropriate responses to these changes are those, which support and encourage this release and peaceful transition. [14]

If they die today, are they ready to meet Jesus?

When a person is not spiritually ready and has unresolved issues, or perhaps they have yet to reconcile certain relationships, he or she may tend to linger to finish the task. The process of dying happens in a way that is unique and appropriate for the values, beliefs, and lifestyle of the dying person. Therefore, as you seek to prepare yourself as the event approaches, you may want to know what to expect and how to respond in ways that will help your loved one accomplish this transition with support, understanding, and ease.

Bedside manners

When communicating with family members in the hospital setting, do not talk about the person in their presence, speak with family and friends privately. Never assume that because the person is unable to respond, that person cannot hear. When speaking to the patient, speak to them directly, normal as if they are still cognizant of their surroundings even though there may be no verbal response. There are many recorded cases where a patient in a coma was able to repeat things that they heard while unconscious.

Things to know about the dying

1. What are their fears?
2. What are their hopes and expectations?
3. What is their unfinished business?

Some of the fears the dying may face

1. Loss of control
2. Loss of personal identity
3. Ceasing to be
4. The unknown
5. What happens after death
6. Loss of relationship
7. Incompleteness or lack of meaning in their lives
8. Being a burden
9. Loneliness
10. The dying process itself

a. Will it be painful
b. How long will it take?
c. Will I be abandoned?
d. Will I lose my dignity?

Some of the Hopes concerns of the dying

1. Getting well and be productive again
2. Die with dignity and be surrounded by caring people
3. To be able to maintain some degree of control
4. To be able to express their needs and feelings openly
5. To be able to manage their pain

Some of Their Unfinished Business

1. Seeing a significant person who is far away
2. Taking one more trip to a special place
3. Completing an unfinished project
4. Providing for loved ones
5. Healing any estrangements; feeling forgiven

HABITS OF EFFECTIVE COMFORTERS

It is a privilege being called to help a hurting friend during a time of crisis. Often words are inadequate to alleviate the pain, anguish, frustration, and sadness as a result of personal loss. However, we can help by comforting and supporting others through our actions during these difficult times. The ministry of death and dying is a highly emotional experience for both the family and the caregiver. The process of watching a loved one go through the dying process is traumatic and life altering, and their stages and elements of the dying process a caregiver must be aware of when providing emotional comfort.

Decreased socialization–At the end-of-life stage, the person who is facing death may choose to limit whom they want to be with as they embrace the end. This is often a sign of preparation, acceptance as the person prepares for his or her death. If you are not included as a part of this inner circle of family and friends at the end of the person's life, it does not mean you are not loved or are unimportant. Rather, you have already fulfilled your final task with them, the final chapter of the story is now closed, and it is the time for you to say "good-bye." If you are a part of the inner circle of family and friends, the person will need your affirmation, support, and permission to take the next step.

Giving permission and saying good-bye -Permitting your loved one to let go is one of the more difficult tasks as it is a natural response for family and friends to want to the person to hang on at the end of life at all costs. The ability to release the dying person from this life provides them with the assurance that is all right to let go whenever they are ready and is one of the greatest and final gifts you can give your loved one. This final gesture of love allows for closure to take place and makes the final release possible. It may be helpful to lay in bed with the person and hold them or to take their hand and say everything you need to say. It may be as simple as "I love you." It may include recounting favorite memories, places, and activities you shared. It may include saying, "I am sorry for things that I have done or difficulties in our relationship." It may also include saying "thank you" Do not be afraid to cry with the person as tears expression of love.[15]

Rules of Conduct

1. Do not say too much, a hug, some tears, and a few words can communicate volumes.
2. Do not offer clichés, such as "I know how you feel" or "You should be grateful it was not worse" or "You must be strong"

or "God will never give you more than you can handle". These may be true, but they are not comforting.

3. Let the person feel the pain. There are many myths surrounding grief, and some people may make statements such as "Bury your feelings," "grieve alone," "Just give it time," "Act like everything is going to be okay and you will get better." We can help end of life survivors recover from their emotional pain by allowing them to go through the grieving process.
4. Let the person talk and share their feelings and pain. If the person says something unexpected, avoid judging or correcting the person. Instead, try to accept what you hear even if you do not understand.
5. Avoid spiritual platitudes. Above all, do not chastise your friend for having less than adequate faith. The person needs for reconciliation with God takes precedence over your concern that he or she might turn away from God. At some point, people are ready to move ahead. Resist the inclination to intervene or protect.
6. Part of the healing process is time, so do not expect the person to be over their loss in a month or even a year or two. Places, music, or a certain smell can trigger a memory, causing the person to lapse back into a state of momentary grief. Holidays and anniversaries will be particularly difficult. So, during these precious moments, be sure to remember the deceased and show extra concern.[16]

Student Notes

Lesson 18

Healing Conversations

Good communication skills are a minister's greatest resource and tool, and if applied properly, can effectively change the lives of the people they minister too. Experts report that what a person says is not as significant on how it is expressed. Extensive research has shown that 90% of communication is nonverbal. Of that 90%, researchers state that 40% of communication involves tone of voice while facial expressions and posture accounts for the remaining 50% of the conversation (Egan, 1976). Healing conversations during times of crisis can create a therapeutic and safe environment for those who are dealing with emotional pain and suffering. The following conversational outline can help set the pace for productive communication.

THERE ARE FOUR (4) STEPS TO THE CONVERSATION PROCESS

STEP ONE FACT – **A non-intrusive inquiry into specifics**

"Where were you when ________?"
"How did you hear about _______?"

STEP TWO THOUGHTS – **encourage linking of facts**

"What did you think when ______?"
What was going through your mind when _____?
"When you look back, what do you think about ________________?"
"Describe any disturbing thoughts about _____?"

STEP THREE – FEELINGS/REACTIONS – **support and encourage**

"I can hear how much you miss_____"
"What touched you the most about__?"
"You seem pretty shaken by _________"
STEP FOUR REASSURANCES – **normalization and education**

"It is okay to cry"
"I am sorry you are having such a difficult time"
"One resource you may want to tap into is _____"

Counselors should remember the following points when counseling the bereaved

1. Confidentiality
2. Use conversational tone
3. The steps above should flow naturally as we are conversing
4. Being present demonstrates you care and want to help.
5. Use good active listening skills.
6. Avoid criticism
7. Humor can be a useful assessment tool
8. Don't lose our cool – get comfortable with anger
9. Problem resolution should not be pushy
10. Allow the bereaved to vent before we provide information or teaching

    If this conversation is being done on the telephone:
11. Avoid call waiting and other distractions
12. Keep background noise to a minimum

13. Use minimal encouragers to make sure they know you are there and listening
14. Some people will open Smore on the phone than in person
15. (There is safety in anonymity) but more difficult for counselors without halo data.

Communicating with those in Grief

When ministering to people who are grieving a personal loss, it is important to refer to the person who has passed away by the name, rather than the deceased. As counselors, we must be cognizant of the fact that the deceased was someone's mother, father, sister, brother, or friend, who influenced the lives of the people who are grieving. Encourage the person who is grieving to share memories.

For example:

- Advice they gave us
- Something they said or did that touched us
- Virtues, achievements, successes for which they'll be remembered
- Do not be afraid to express your own sense of loss
- Do not worry about making the griever cry
- DO SAY
- "It is a great sorrow for us all"
- "I feel fortunate to have known…."
- "I feel the loss of ……"
- "I am greatly saddened by …."
- "Please accept my/our sincere condolences/sympathy"
- "My heart / prayers /thoughts /sympathies are with you and your family"
- "He or she will be long remembered for."
- "I feel privileged to have counted (name) as a friend"
- "While no words of mine can ease your loss, I just wanted you to know that I am grieving with you and your family"

Be careful of Clichés

Many people who have received condolences from others during a time of personal loss have been the recipient of some of the well-meaning but hurtful clichés, false cheerfulness, and optimistic platitudes that pass for expressions of sympathy. Counselors should keep in mind the following guidelines in what not to say or ask, so we can avoid burdening the bereaved with painful verbiage. Avoid excessive dramatic language ("dreadful, horrible, appalling news." Avoid pious clichés, simplistic explanations, or interpretations of God's intents or involvement in this sorrowful event.

- Do not give advice
- Avoid generic offers of help
- Be specific

NEVER SAY

- "I know just how you feel"
- "Be happy for what you have"
- "Are you over it yet?"
- "Don't cry"
- "Life is for the living"
- "He/she was too young to die"
- "At least you had him/her for twenty years"
- "I feel almost worse than you do"
- "God had a purpose in sending you this burden, you are stronger now"

NO NEED TO REASSURE

- "At least his/her suffering is over"
- "He/she is in a better place now"
- "You'll feel better soon. It takes time, that's all"
- "Be brave"

- "Life must go on. Time heals all wounds. You'll feel better before you know it"
- "Thank God you have other children"

Chaplaincy is a unique aspect of Christian ministry that will send you on a journey beyond the walls of the church into the world of hurting people. Many of the people whom you will come into contact may never grace the door of a church, meaning you may be the only connection to the church and God the person may ever encounter. As a chaplain, you will meet people where they are at in life and minister to them in their environment. You will become part of their lives, community, and industry. I hope that we have been able to open your eyes to the world of chaplaincy.

Student Notes

COUNSELING RECAP

A QUICK TOPIC RECAP AT A GLANCE

Counseling Recap

Information at a Glance

INTRODUCTION | COLLECTING AND ORGANIZING DATA

In this course on Biblical Counseling, we have learned that some of the skills required to be effective counselors are,

1. Listening	2. Observing	Asking appropriate questions

The forms included here are useful for gather vital information about the person we are counseling. The amount of information we get from the counselee can be overwhelming at times, and it is up to you as the counselor to collect and organize this data in a way that will be helpful in the counseling process.

Note taking when it is appropriate

It is recommended that note taking be done sparingly during the actual counseling sessions – you should be focused on listening to the counselee. It is difficult to carry on an in-depth conversation or establish a connection with someone when you are busy writing. That said there are tools and techniques that can be used to aid the counselor in gathering the information critical to the counseling process.

Counselors should jot down important phrases, statements, or ideas, which can help him, recollect, reflect, and evaluate the session later. After each session, the counselor should take a few minutes to record any comments or significant pieces of information. This would also be a good time to begin planning for the next session. The importance of becoming skilled in taking inventory cannot be overestimated. To a large degree, the entire Biblical counseling process depends on it.

The Kind of Information to Collect

Systematically collecting and organizing information can help counselors be thorough. For example, by organizing information into different categories, counselors can see many aspects of a counselee's life and assess how they influence each other and the counselee's particular problem(s). This can also help counselors point to specific areas of a counselee's life that might be of particular importance.

We will briefly explore six areas that could affect a counselee's ability to address/resolve their problems. As counselors, we need to focus on gathering information about these areas:

1. Physical Condition
2. Spiritual Condition
3. Emotional Condition
4. Action/Inaction
5. Concept

COLLECTING AND ORGANIZING DATA

Physical Condition

Physical problems can both contribute to and be a result of spiritual problems. The success of our counsel will sometimes be dependent upon understanding a particular aspect of someone's health. Thus, we need to be aware of any physical problems of our counselees if we desire to help solve the inward problems they face. There are five (5) aspects of our physical lives that can influence our spiritual health.

(1) Sleep	(2) Diet	(3) Exercise	(4) Illness	(5) Medications

Irregular sleep patterns is often linked to spiritually related issues that can lead to anxiety, guilt, or a lack of desire to participate in day to day activities. The average person needs approximately seven to eight hours of sleep per night. Chronic sleep deprivation is often a contributing factor to depression. An adequate amount of sleep is crucial for good and healthy mental health.

Diet - Nutritional imbalance can affect emotional behavior. As stated in the old adage, "you are what you eat." If the person appears to be on-edged, nervous, or is experiencing bouts of hyperactive, an enquiry should be made about the person's daily routine as well as their intake of stimulants such as caffeine, sugar, or other drugs. We must not ignore the diet factor in our counseling sessions as it may reveal important information about the person's state of mind.

Exercise - Lack of exercise can contribute to heighten levels of anxiety and stress. Recommending an exercise regimen can significantly help the counselee to relieve stress and anxiety, boost energy, and create a sense of wellbeing.

Illness – Illnesses can play a role in a person's physical and emotional disposition, which can lead to depression, stomach ulcers, gastric disturbances, and other ailments. The abuse of drugs and alcohol can also be a contributing factor. There are moments when the counselees should be urged to seek medical attention, receive a proper diagnosis and treatment before starting a counseling session.

Medications - Various types of over the counter and prescription medications can cause harmful side effects. These drugs can be a contributing factor when it comes to chronic physical and emotional problems, especially if the individual is not aware of the possibility of side effects. Some cases of mild depression, for example, may be solved simply by finding out what medication the person has been taking and whether it might be causing side effects that are contributing to the depression. If prescription medication appears to result in a behavioral side effect, refer the counselee back to the prescribing physician.

Spiritual Condition - Early in the counseling process, it is important for counselor to ascertain a person's spiritual condition, which is important when providing Biblical based counseling. If the person you are counseling is not a Christian, at the very least, the principles of Biblical based counseling can still be applied. Additionally, understanding the counselee's circle of influence, such as church, family, and friends can have a direct impact on the person's recovery.

Emotional State - Counselors should never ignore counselee's emotional state. We must recognize the significance of emotions because they are God-given outward indicators of what is happening in a human heart and are often linked to the problems people face. It is very important to ascertain specific triggers that may bring on certain emotions in the counselee, for example, certain events, people, objects, activities, or memories.

Action and Inaction - Counselors need to consider what the person has done regarding their circumstances and what they failed to do. Actions have a profound effect on a person's spiritual, emotional, and physical health. Actions of disobedience can affect a person's relationship with God, produce various negative emotions, and lead to further sinful actions against others and self. The "way" of life requires obedience to the commands in God's Word, and the way of death is assured by disobedience to them. *Thus said the Lord: "Behold, I set before you the way if life and the way of death." (Jeremiah 21:8)*

Heart Condition – The Bible teaches that the *Word of God is living and powerful, and sharper than a two-edged sword, piercing even the division of the soul and spirit, and of joint, and marrow, and is a discerner of the thoughts and intentions of the heart. (Hebrews 4:12)*

Concepts include,

- 🕮 Personal Convictions
- 🕮 Attitudes
- 🕮 Who and what are they relying upon?
- 🕮 Expectations
- 🕮 Desires
- 🕮 Values

The word of Jesus tells us, No *one can serve two masters; for either he will hate the one and love the other, or else he will be loyal to the one and despise the other. You cannot serve God and mammon. [Refers to wealth, money, or property] (Mathews 6:24)*

Jesus says that sin is an inner problem, one that runs much deeper than the surface behavior. It is in the hearts and minds of people. It is the inner part of us that influences how we will act or what we will say. This dimension of life must be addressed if lasting change is to take place. Often, many counselors become frustrated with the person they are trying to help because they only see a temporary change in the life of the individual. In such instances the counselees return to the same lifestyle shortly after their session. In most cases, the reason for the failure is that the minds and hearts of those people have not experienced true spiritual renewal and past influences often play a role in a person's relapse. If we want to practice true biblical counseling, we must gain as much information as we can about the person, their thoughts, and desires so we can correct their misconceptions and help them to have "the mind of Christ" concerning their problems (cf. 1 Corinthians 2:16)

Personal History – The term personal history refers to the individual's personal data both past and present, the influences, circumstances, and experiences that govern their lifestyle and the way in which they deal with life in general. Issues that need to be addressed include family origin, marital history, and other significant relationships, problems that may be rooted in school or family, and possible physical or sexual abuse. We need to be concerned about any shaping experiences from the past – especially those that the counselee believes are important. The counselor must pay attention to those people who struggle with a chronic preoccupation with the past, struggling with personal traumas that have shaped the way they in which they deal with the present.

We cannot ignore the past regardless how painful it may be because the past often establishes a lasting pattern of conduct that can diametrically affect the person ability to cope with current problems and situations, especially if it involves a continuous pattern of sin. As counselors we should listen attentively to their story, identify with the pain they have suffered, then lovingly and patiently help them acknowledge the origin of their struggle and encourage take action to address the issue. We must consider the sensitive and personal nature of the history of those we counsel, if for no other reason than it is important to them. If we demonstrate a lack of concern, it will hinder the counselor/counselee relationship.

CONGRATULATIONS YOU ARE DONE

IN THE LINE OF DUTY FORMS SAMPLES

Many emergency services, prisons and healthcare providers provide their chaplains with forms that are exclusive to their setting. Some agencies do not supply their chaplains with the paperwork or means to document their activities while on duty. In any case, it is important to document your activities whether responding to an independent callout or serving with an agency in the line of duty. You may be called upon to testify in court. Should the occasion arise, good documentation of your activities will be of vital importance. You may design your own forms, or you may purchase our templates through Chaplains International, Inc. 13061 Rosedale Hwy. G141, Bakersfield, CA 93314 / (888) 627-5503 / www.chaplainsinternationalinc.com

Valuable Resources

The following are some national assistance organizations that may be of service during a time of need. We strongly recommend that you become acquainted with your local metal health department, mortuaries, and public assistance agencies as they can provide information and care that is relevant to your community needs.

Sudden Infant Death Syndrome (SIDS) Alliance
1314 Bedford Ave. Suite, 210
Baltimore, MD 21208
Phone: (410) 653-8709
Fax: (410) 653-8709
Web: http://www.sidsalliance.org.

American Association of Suicidology
4201 Connecticut Ave. NW Suite 408
Washington, DC 20008
Phone: (202) 237-2280
Fax: (202 237-2282
Web: http://www.suicidology.org

National Organization for Victim Assistance
1757 Park Road, NW
Washington, DC 20010
Phone: (202) 232-6683
Fax: (202) 462-2255
Web: http://try-nova.org

Violence Prevention Program
Harvard School of Public Health
718 Huntington Ave, 1st Floor
Boston, MA 02115
Phone: (617) 432-0814
Fax: (617) 432-0068

Tragedy Assistance Program for Survivors (TAPS)
2001 S Street, NW, #300
Washington, DC 20009

Mothers Against Drunk Driving (MADD)
511 E. John Carpenter Freeway, Suite 700
Irving, TX 75062
Phone: (214) 744-6233
Victim hot line: (800) GET-MADD
Fax: (972) 529-5300
Web: http://www.madd.org

List of Contributors

Paul Mikus, M.A., Th.D.
Adjunct Professor at Chaplains College School of Graduate Studies

Norberto Guzmán, M.C.C.
Adjunct Professor at Chaplains College School of Graduate Studies, Signet Bible College, and Theological Seminary

Edward Ehee, M.A.
Advisor on course development for Chaplains College School of Graduate Studies

Vu Lee, M.D.
Advisor on course development for Chaplains College School of Graduate Studies

Chaplains International, Inc.,
publisherof the following books, ***The Chaplaincy*** and ***Invasion of the Cults*** want to offer you a

TRAINING OPPORTUNITY

Earn your Certification today!

Self-study at your own pace

The CTI Certification Course is a self-study program that includes book and video lectures, as well as reusable resources that will aid you through the study process. As a CTI student, you will learn the basics of chaplaincy from chaplains with real world experience. This program is valuable for people who have no formal chaplain training, but who are ministering within the prison system, conduct hospital and hospice care visits, or provide community support in a religious setting, as well as churches who are interested in incorporating chaplaincy as part of their outreach ministry program. Perhaps you are an experienced chaplain looking for refresher training. We can help enroll today!

FOR MORE INFORMATION CONTACT US

Phone: (888) 627-5503
Email: chaplain2000@aol.com
ChaplainsInternationalInc.com

Other books by Dale Scadron

Invasion of the Cults

Be ready to defend your faith and do so with confidence.
Pick up a copy at your favorite bookstore or order
a copy online at Barnes and Nobel or Amazon.

Special Thanks
to our Resource Providers

Endnotes

1 By (CI) Chaplain Norberto Guzman, B.A., M.C.C. / Signet Bible College and Theological Seminary

2 https://www.coursehero.com/file/36977813/Ferguson-docx/

3 https://bcnn1wp.wordpress.com/2017/09/29/listen-first-responder-chaplaincy-part-5-ordained-chaplains-work-of-the-chaplain-54-with-daniel-whyte-iii-gospel-light-society-university/

4 https://ffc.wildapricot.org/Resources/Documents/Resources/Beginning%20a%20Fire%20Chaplaincy.pdf

5 https://bcnn1wp.wordpress.com/2017/07/19/listen-correctional-and-prison-chaplaincy-part-7-ordained-chaplains-work-of-the-chaplain-49-with-daniel-whyte-iii-gospel-light-society-university/

6 https://bcnn1wp.wordpress.com/2017/07/19/listen-correctional-and-prison-chaplaincy-part-7-ordained-chaplains-work-of-the-chaplain-49-with-daniel-whyte-iii-gospel-light-society-university/

7 https://iuhealth.org/for-media/press-releases/iu-health-frankfort-hospital-appoints-new-chaplain

8 https://www.change-career-with-purpose.com/hospicechaplainduties.html

9 T5360.02 Ministry of a BOP Chaplain / Technical Reference Manual

10 National Sheriffs Association – Chaplains Reference Guide

11 National Sheriffs Association – Chaplains Reference Guide

12 https://s3.amazonaws.com/media.cloversites.com/76/763db47d-19eb-456a-9515-30e97f759a5f/documents/Class_9_PBC_-_Forgiveness.pdf

13 https://www.simonandschuster.com/books/The-7-Habits-of-Highly-Effective-People/Stephen-R-Covey/9781451639612

14 http://www.palliativecarensw.org.au/pdfs/PCNSW-Signs-Symptoms-of-Approaching-Death-ARTICLE.pdf

15 http://www.craigscause.ca/page.asp?ID=44

16 http://archive.signalscv.com/archives/925/

CPSIA information can be obtained
at www.ICGtesting.com
Printed in the USA
BVHW091244180722
642397BV00013BA/418